GREAT BRITAIN AND
GERMANY'S LOST COLONIES

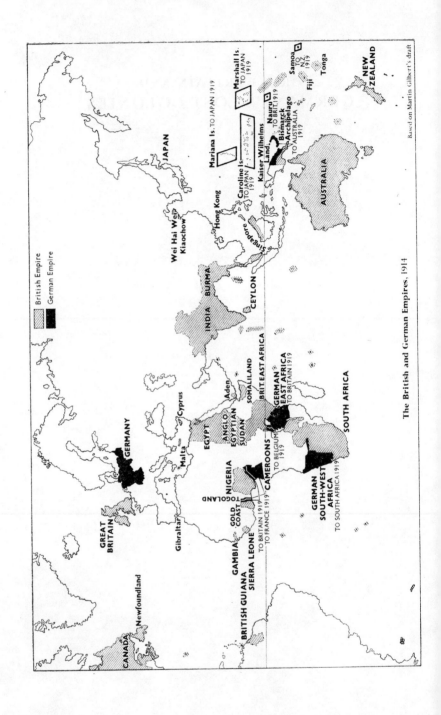

The British and German Empires, 1914

Based on Martin Gilbert's draft

British Empire
German Empire

GREAT BRITAIN
GERMANY
JAPAN
Newfoundland
CANADA
Gibraltar
Malta
Cyprus
EGYPT
ANGLO EGYPTIAN SUDAN
Aden
SOMALILAND
BRIT EAST AFRICA
GAMBIA
SIERRA LEONE
NIGERIA
GOLD COAST
TOGOLAND
TO BRITAIN 1919
TO FRANCE 1919
CAMEROONS
TO BELGIUM 1919
GERMAN EAST AFRICA
TO BRITAIN 1919
GERMAN SOUTH-WEST AFRICA
TO SOUTH AFRICA 1919
SOUTH AFRICA
BRITISH GUIANA
INDIA
BURMA
CEYLON
Wei Hai Wei
Kiaochow
Hong Kong
Singapore
Mariana Is. TO JAPAN 1919
Caroline Is. TO JAPAN 1919
Marshall Is. TO JAPAN 1919
Kaiser Wilhelms Land
Bismarck Archipelago TO AUSTRALIA 1919
Nauru TO BRIT. 1919
AUSTRALIA
Samoa TO NZ 1919
Fiji
Tonga
NEW ZEALAND

GREAT BRITAIN
AND
GERMANY'S
LOST COLONIES

1914–1919

BY

WM. ROGER LOUIS

CLARENDON PRESS
OXFORD
1967

Oxford University Press, Ely House, London W.1

GLASGOW NEW YORK TORONTO MELBOURNE WELLINGTON
CAPE TOWN SALISBURY IBADAN NAIROBI LUSAKA ADDIS ABABA
BOMBAY CALCUTTA MADRAS KARACHI LAHORE DACCA
KUALA LUMPUR HONG KONG TOKYO

PRINTED AND BOUND IN ENGLAND BY
HAZELL WATSON AND VINEY LTD
AYLESBURY, BUCKS

To A. J. P. Taylor

PREFACE

THIS book aims to relate succinctly the history of British policy towards the German colonies from 1914 to 1919 and to quote fully from newly available evidence on the subject. The basic sources are the documents of the Foreign Office, Colonial Office and War Cabinet at the Public Record Office, London. To make clear how I have used them, a word needs to be said about how British policy was shaped during the war. Until the establishment of the War Cabinet in December 1916, long range political policy—as distinct from military policy, with which this book is not directly concerned—was formed by inter-departmental groups (Foreign Office, Colonial Office, India Office, War Office, Admiralty, and Board of Trade) appointed by the Committee of Imperial Defence or by the Cabinet (which itself only rarely considered the question and whose records until December 1916 are incomplete). Immediate decisions were taken by the Foreign Office and Colonial Office, sometimes after consultation with the southern Dominions of South Africa, Australia and New Zealand. Relatively full accounts of the policy making process in regard to the West and East African campaigns, which were controlled from London, may be found in the Colonial Office and Foreign Office files; but, in other theatres where the Dominions were in charge of the operations, the development of British policy also has to be traced through the records preserved in the Union Archives at Pretoria, the Commonwealth Archives Office in Canberra, and the New Zealand Archives in Wellington. After December 1916 all of those sources, especially the Foreign Office and Colonial Office files, continue to fill in many important details; but the main sources of information then come from the very full series of War Cabinet papers (especially the 'G.', 'G.T.', 'P.' and 'W.C.P.' series—all classified at the Public Record Office under various CAB. references), and minutes of the War Cabinet and Imperial War Cabinet which record discussions and decisions. Full references to those are given in the footnotes of the text. I must thank the Public Record Office and the archivists of the other collections mentioned above for permission to quote from official documents.

Even with the vast amount of official material now accessible at the Public Record Office, the full history of British policy towards the German colonies cannot be told without reference to several extremely valuable collections of private papers. During the first part of the war important business was often transacted through private correspondence, and the Harcourt Papers at Stanton Harcourt (by kind permission of Lord Harcourt) contain a whole range of information about British policy not to be found at the Public Record Office. The same is true of the papers of Lord Novar (Sir Ronald Munro Ferguson, who once wrote that his private letters were 'the chief records of events in Australia'), and to a lesser extent of two other collections at the Australian National Library, the papers of J. G. Latham and William M. Hughes (I wish to thank Sir Archie Grenfell Price, Harold L. White and L. F. Fitzhardinge for help in regard to these Australian collections). The private papers of General J. C. Smuts at the University of Cape Town (made available to me by kind permission of Sir Keith Hancock and the Smuts Archive Trust) are fundamental. The papers of the Anti-Slavery and Aborigines Protection Society (Rhodes House, Oxford) are the main unpublished source of information about the development of the trusteeship idea in non-official circles. The Milner Papers (Bodleian Library, Oxford) are essential for a complete account of the colonial settlement at the Peace Conference. Other collections such as the Asquith Papers (Bodleian Library) and the Austen Chamberlain Papers (University of Birmingham), and other collections of marginal use referred to occasionally in the footnotes of the text, have lost much of their novelty in view of the opening of new material at the Public Record Office; but I have given references to them if they contain related important material. I hope my indebtedness to the owners and archivists of the collections mentioned above will be apparent. I wish to thank the Cabinet Office for permitting me to use and publish official material found in private papers.

'The essential matter of history', Maitland once wrote, 'is not what happened but what people thought or said about it'. Private letters and official documents alone by no means provide the key to understanding the colonial issue during the war, and in an attempt to comprehend the feeling of moral revulsion felt by the British public towards the atrocities allegedly committed by the Germans in the colonies, I have tried to make a wide study of the daily press—usually the best way in which an historian can truly grasp the spirit of the times. As before the war, British humanitarian zeal to right European colonial wrongs united tories and radicals alike, with only a small body of dissenting sceptics remaining outside the main stream of public opinion. Germany's 'colonial guilt' became apparent to most Englishmen almost from the outbreak of the war. If the Germans committed atrocities in Belgium, it seemed clear that they must have done even more appalling things in Africa. In due course the Government provided official evidence of Germany's maladministration in the colonies by publishing several Blue Books on the subject. Here the new evidence reveals little that has not been known before. In the pre-war pattern, the Blue Books were prepared in the department most directly concerned with the question, in this case usually by the Colonial Office, but with Foreign Office collaboration. Despatches were reproduced, giving the impression of historical accuracy; but as before the war, objectionable passages which might throw the Government in an unfavourable light were rewritten or simply omitted—in one Colonial Secretary's euphemistic phrase, 'edited up to our standard'. They have little historical value other than as an example of war time propaganda and as one of the causes of Germany's reputation as a brutal and cruel colonial power.

Still, the Blue Books form one of the main sources used by historians who have dealt with the problem until now. Other traditional sources, such as wartime books on the German colonies, have also been used many times by other historians and are not emphasized here. A full discussion of books and a list of doctoral dissertations which bear on the subject may be found in a bibliographical chapter by Alison Smith and Hartmut Pogge-von Strandmann in *Imperial Rivalry and Colonial Rule: Britain and Germany in Africa* (forthcoming), and in my essay, 'Great Britain and International Trusteeship: the Mandate System', in *The Historiography of the British Empire-Commonwealth*, edited by Robin W. Winks. The very extensive and detailed official histories of the military operations in the German colonies remain indispensable. They cover the ground so fully that in the present study I have given only the briefest summary of the military campaigns in order to concentrate on the broader political aspects of the question.

The documents on which this book is based represent, in my opinion, the essential evidence necessary for a study of British colonial aims during the First World War. But a word of caution needs to be said about any argument, such as this one, which contends that there were in fact any definable colonial aims, or, in a wider sense, war aims. Only a small number of British statesmen gave even relative priority to colonial problems during the war, and none of them urged the expansion of the British Empire as a goal desirable in itself. The arguments put forward in favour of retaining the German colonies were perhaps even more complex than similar ones of the late nineteenth century, and rested on relatively sophisticated premises of strategic necessity and humanitarian duty. If public statements made by British politicians during the war are to be believed, the latter consideration motivated British policy. At the Peace Conference 'the magic of the word "mandate" ', as Miss Elizabeth Monroe has written in her brilliant work, *Britain's Moment in the Middle East* (London, 1963), transformed the German colonies into territories held in sacred trust for civilization, and did much to disarm critics who denounced Britain for grabbing most of the colonial spoils. Until recently the problem of knowing the precise spoils which the British Government regarded as the most valuable has been largely a matter of guesswork. The archives now reveal that governmental committees wrote lengthy reports on the subject during the course of the war. Even those formal and precise statements, however, should not be interpreted as the final colonial aims of the British Government. As the Prime Minister, Lloyd George, said at the close of the war, all reports and decisions could still be revised. Nevertheless there are certain recurrent themes and evaluations—discussed at length in the text—which together may be taken as an explanation of what the British aimed to achieve in the colonial world. The aims were far from modest. Once intoxicated with the possibility of painting more of the map red, as the Secretary of State for India, E. S. Montagu, once said, it was difficult to find 'some convincing argument for not annexing all the territories in the world'.

*   *   *

For such a modest work as this there are numerous people who have had to suffer its completion, not least my wife and colleagues in the Department of History of Yale University. Among the latter I am especially indebted to Professors Harry R. Rudin, Hans W. Gatzke, Gaddis Smith and Robin W. Winks. In a similar way I am grateful for suggestions I have received from Professors Arthur S. Link and Richard H. Ullman of Princeton and Ernest R. May of Harvard, and for the very perceptive criticism of Professor Jean Stengers of the University of Brussels. I also wish to take this opportunity to acknowledge valuable assistance given me in various ways by Professors John A. Gallagher, Sir Keith Hancock, Lawrence E. Gelfand, Hans A. Schmitt; Hartmut Pogge-von Strandmann, Suzanne Miers, David Goldey, Sally Chilver, Ralph Austen, and especially Alison Smith. I must further thank the editors of the *American Historical Review*, the *Journal of Modern History* and *African Affairs* for permitting me to draw upon material presented in a different context in the pages of those journals. A Junior Faculty Fellowship arranged by the Concilium on International Studies of Yale University made the research for this and other studies possible, and I am immensely grateful to Professor Arthur F. Wright in that regard. During my leave of absence I once again enjoyed the generous hospitality of the Warden and Fellows of St. Antony's College, Oxford, and I wish especially to thank Professor Kenneth Kirkwood, Miss Elizabeth Monroe and Geoffrey Hudson, who have criticized the manuscript from their respective vantage points of Africa, the Middle East and Far East. To Miss Agatha Ramm of Somerville College, Oxford, I owe a good deal of what I know about the use of historical evidence, and I hope that my handling of the documents on which this book is based reflects in small measure the skill and exactitude with which she has patiently corrected so many of my writings. As usual I am finally indebted to A. J. P. Taylor. When I asked him how to go about writing this book, he said 'just tell the story briefly and try to make it detached, precise and rather dull'. Having many times received similar good advice and criticism from him, I take the opportunity to dedicate this book to one of the most provocative and great historians of our time.

CONTENTS

INTRODUCTION

IN 1919 the problem of Germany, above all, loomed over the Paris Peace Conference. At that time no less than in the late nineteenth and mid-twentieth centuries the representatives of the British Government puzzled over the conundrum of how to deal with a large and at times extremely powerful state that had more than once threatened to conquer Europe. Three main and to some extent inseparable solutions dominated British thought. The first was to disarm Germany and to ensure that she would remain militarily impotent. The second was to build or create states such as Poland, Czechoslovakia and Yugoslavia as barriers to German expansion. The third was to strip Germany of her overseas possessions and thereby secure the safety of the 'Southern British World' as well as of the Empire as a whole. That last consideration, which during the war became complicated by Bolshevik propaganda and Wilsonian idealism, forms the theme of this book.

To those not involved in imperial affairs, the German colonial issue seemed only a minor one. As President Wilson is reported to have said at the Peace Conference, 'the disposition of the German Colonies was not vital to the life of the world in any respect. It was the determination of the pressing European questions which was all-important'.[1] Nor was the issue directly connected with the main events of the war—as may be easily gathered from the way accounts of the colonial campaigns are usually tucked away in the back of military histories as if irrelevant. None of the 'side shows' had any impact on the outcome of the war except in the negative sense of prolonging it by the depletion of Allied resources. As Bismarck had anticipated thirty years earlier, colonial questions during wartime would not be settled in the colonies 'but by fighting in the central theatre of war'. According to General Sir James E. Edmonds in his summary of the British military histories, 'The operations in the "side shows", in Mesopotamia, Egypt, and Palestine, and in the German colonies ... had no direct

[1] *Papers relating to the Foreign Relations of the United States: the Paris Peace Conference, 1919* (13 vols., Washington, 1942–47), III, p. 771.

military effect on the struggle in the main theatre, except the absorption of British man-power, British material, and British convoy power . . . '.[2] That statement represents the consensus of historical opinion on the subject, and from a military point of view is no doubt accurate. But it by no means reflects the geo-political importance attached to the colonial issue by British statesmen who believed that German gains in Europe could be offset only by the consolidation and expansion of the British Empire overseas. The high priests of that doctrine were Lewis Harcourt (Colonial Secretary until May 1915), and three members of the War Cabinet (from December 1916), Lord Curzon, General J. C. Smuts of South Africa, and Lord Milner. To them the war was being fought, above all, to achieve the security of the Empire—a goal, so far as they were concerned, that could not be attained without the elimination of the German colonies.

Their reasoning is easy to follow. Until the last months of the war, it seemed entirely possible that Germany would emerge from the struggle as the master of Europe whose next ambition would be global hegemony. But only with colonies as bases for submarines and airplanes, and with the help of African man-power, would Germany be able to bid for world conquest. Without an overseas Empire, Germany could be contained in Europe, perhaps by deflecting her aggression eastwards towards Russia—the idea in Milner's mind when at various times he considered the possibility of a negotiated peace.[3] If, on the other hand, Germany were allowed to retain her colonies and also absorb the Belgian and Portuguese colonies in Africa, she would splinter the developing system of communications of the British Empire and would be given, theoretically at least, not only a military base from which to menace all parts of the world, but also the resources of tropical Africa with which to outpace the Allies in industrial development. Above all, she would have at her disposal the human material to build a huge 'black army'. This interpretation of German war aims held, in short, that the Germans intended to create a central African Empire

---

[2] Sir James E. Edmonds, *A Short History of World War I* (London, 1951), p. ix.

[3] In this connection see A. M. Gollin, *Proconsul in Politics: a Study of Lord Milner in Opposition and in Power* (London, 1964), chap. XX.

stretching from the Atlantic to the Indian ocean—a *Mittel-afrika*—as a base to paralyze Allied shipping and commerce, to extend German influence even to South America and Australasia, and eventually to mobilize black Africans in order to aid her conquest of the world. To prove the grim determination with which the Germans pursued that aim, the British press often quoted a comment by one of the prominent German publicists, Emil Zimmermann, '*We are fighting for a Central African Empire*'.

Since there is no comprehensive study of German colonial aims,[4] it is difficult to say how much the British exaggerated the danger of *Mittelafrika* and mistook the utterances of fire-eating journalists for the policy of the German Government. But it is clear that, as German publicists shifted their attention from the visionary scheme of *Mitteleuropa* to the ones of Berlin to Baghdad and *Mittelafrika*, the British were able to make of German war aims whatever suited their fancy. To those concerned with colonial affairs and the security of the Empire at large, the colonial danger seemed paramount. L. S. Amery, Milner's disciple and one of the secretaries of the War Cabinet, powerfully stated the case in 1917:

The object of British policy can still be defined, as Pitt defined it in the great revolutionary war, by the one word "security"—the maintenance of such external conditions as will permit the peaceful development of British institutions. . . . It is this continuous creation of new sources of power in new worlds oversea to redress the balance of the Old World which is the really characteristic feature of British policy, and accounts for the fact that an essentially defensive policy has led to the acquisition of immense Empire. . . .
The . . . German policy, that of sea power and colonial expansion at the expense of the British Empire, is, for the moment, defeated. But if Germany can recover her colonies, or even add to them as she hopes, by the annexation of Portuguese colonies, or by the control of the Congo, she will be able to renew it with far greater hopes of

---

[4] But see Fritz Fischer, *Griff nach der Weltmacht* (3rd edn., Düsseldorf, 1964), chap. XXII. There is also an article by H. Stoecker, 'Bemerkungen über die deutschen Kriegsziele in Afrika südlich der Sahara', *Wissenschaftliche Zeitschrift der Humboldt-Universität, Gesellschafts und Sprachwissenschaftliche Reihe*, 13 (Berlin, 1964). Noteworthy dissertations on the subject are by D. Kersten (Hamburg, 1963); A. Rüger (Humboldt-Universität, Berlin, 1964); Robert L. Bradford (Yale University, 1965) and A. W. Lever (University of Wisconsin, 1963). The last work is especially important because it systematically discusses the published material in English.

success. She will take effective military measures to make her colonies secure against conquest, and she will establish in each of them bases for submarines and raiders. A base in Duala in the Cameroons, commanding the routes to South America and South Africa; a base in East Africa, whose radius covered the entrance to the Red Sea and threatened all communications between India and South Africa; one or more bases in the Pacific—once they are well organized the next war with the British Empire could be undertaken under far more favourable conditions.[5]

The developments in air and submarine warfare and other technological advances seemed to make *every* German colony a potential menace. At the close of the Napoleonic wars, the British could return colonial territories to France because supremacy of British sea power nullified any great danger from a colonial quarter. But a hundred years later they refused to return even the smallest colony, Togoland, to Germany.

The changing nature of warfare seemed to enhance the value of British communications and resuscitated the Cape to Cairo and other visions of the late 1880s. The main line of speculation ran as follows. If Germany were to win the war, or even if she were to lose and then rebuild her navy—and if there were continued technological advances—German submarines might eventually command the seas. In view of the British strategy of the 'long haul', by which they eventually won wars by powerful coalitions and colonial support,[6] that could be disastrous unless Britain could hold open her lines of communication with North America and her African, Indian and Australasian empires. In Africa the key was German East Africa. If Britain permanently were to acquire that colony, there would be a continuous stretch of British territory from South Africa to Egypt—from the Cape to Cairo. Airplanes would be able to fly from London to Pretoria in a matter of days. In time of war troops could be moved overland by rail or road the length of the continent; and in time of peace the British would be able to develop the resources of the backbone of the continent. With large parts of the Middle East also falling under British sway, communica-

[5] Memorandum by Amery, 'Notes on Possible Terms of Peace', G.T.-448, Secret, 11 Apr. 1917, CAB. 24/10.
[6] See Noble Frankland, 'Britain's Changing Strategic Position', *International Affairs*, XXXIII (Oct. 1957).

tions would be open to India and on to Australasia. In short, the extension of British influence over parts of the Turkish empire, together with the destruction of Germany's colonial system, would strengthen the British Empire and inaugurate a new era of the *Pax Britannica* in the southern hemisphere. In that context the old slogans of 'Cape to Cairo' and 'Cairo to Calcutta' acquired a new meaning. To use different clichés, even though Europe might fall under the Prussian boot, the banner of freedom would still fly in the southern British hemisphere. In retrospect some of those ideas may seem fantastical, but they were no more removed from reality than those put forward by the German colonial visionaries.

By the close of 1916 the conquest of the German colonies was virtually complete, though the Germans in East Africa did not lay down their arms until after the armistice. The German possessions in the Far East were seized by Australasian and Japanese forces, South-West Africa by the South Africans, Togoland and the Cameroons by an Anglo-French contingent, and German East Africa by British and Belgian troops. With the French and the Japanese the British entered into secret agreements for the provisional partition and administration of the conquered territories. As in the case of the Allied secret agreement of 1915 about the Straits and the Sykes-Picot agreement of 1916 that partitioned the Middle East into various shades of British and French influence, these arrangements were designed as much to prevent misunderstanding and to promote cooperation as they were to parcel out the spoils. Where possible the British delayed entering into secret territorial agreements as long as they could, and not until February 1917, at a time when additional Japanese naval assistance was urgently needed, did they agree to support Japanese claims in Shantung and the German islands north of the Equator. They refused point blank to recognize Belgian claims in East Africa. To the Italians, on the other hand, they promised in the Treaty of London of 1915 to provide 'equitable compensation' if the Allies extended their colonial empires at Germany's expense. In the end the British had to give the Belgians more than the Italians because Belgian troops actually occupied German colonial territory and there was no way to expel them short of force.

The British Government did not regard this renewed colonial

scramble as 'imperialism' at work. In fact the word was seldom used except when describing the motives of the French and the Italians. In one of the few official commentaries on the notion of economic imperialism, Curzon wrote in 1917 merely that 'the epithet "imperialism", like the epithet "capitalistic", has become one of the cant formulas of the doctrinaires of revolution'.[7] There were in Britain certain bodies—such as the Empire Resources Development Committee, a group dedicated to the application of Leopoldian principles to Northern Rhodesia by appropriating 'vacant lands'—which were bent on the economic exploitation of colonial territories; but, so far as those who shaped British policy were concerned, it would be much more accurate to apply the old-fashioned definition of an 'imperialist' as one who for reasons of strategy or prestige wanted to expand the Empire, rather than to regard them as motivated by the economic principles attacked by Hobson and Lenin.

So powerful was the catch phrase 'no annexations' released by the Russian revolution and supported by President Wilson, that the British Government felt it necessary to prove that its policy towards the German colonies was not motivated by an urge for territorial aggrandizement—in Amery's phrase, that the British Empire was not 'a land devouring octopus'. In January 1918 the Prime Minister proclaimed at Smuts's suggestion that the principle of self-determination was as applicable to the populations of the German colonies as to the ones of Europe. The War Cabinet had confidence that the 'natives'[8] would opt for British rule. In the frank words of Lord Curzon:

I am inclined to value the argument of self-determination because I believe that most of the people would determine in our favour. . . . if we cannot get out of our difficulties in any other way we ought to play self-determination for all it is worth wherever we are involved in difficulties with the French, the Arabs, or anybody else, and leave the case to be settled by that final argument knowing in the bottom of our hearts that we are more likely to benefit from it than anybody else.[9]

[7] Memorandum by Curzon, 'German and Turkish Territories Captured in the War', Secret, G.-182, 5 Dec. 1917, CAB. 24/4.

[8] Throughout this book I have used the word 'native' because it was the term used by those who dealt with colonial questions during the First World War.

[9] Eastern Committee Minutes, Secret, 5 Dec. 1918, CAB. 27/24.

'Self-determination' eventually became embodied in Article 22 of the League Covenant, the charter of the mandates system—a triumph for President Wilson, but one regarded by Allied statesmen as meaningless so far as the German colonies were concerned.

During the last part of the war the main problem facing the British in regard to the future colonial settlement was this: how to achieve security without alienating the United States. To allay President Wilson's suspicions of British 'imperialism', the members of the War Cabinet proclaimed themselves in favour of 'mandates', a device by which conquered enemy territories would be held not as possessions but as 'sacred trusts'. They decided that the United States should be invited to participate in this experiment. Anglo-American cooperation in colonial affairs would help to stabilize the non-European world; and the 'mandates' in fact would differ only in name from other colonial possessions. In the event the Americans did not accept mandates and persevered in their traditional suspicion of European colonial ventures; and the Permanent Mandates Commission of the League of Nations, and its successor body, the Trusteeship Council of the United Nations, helped to carry many of the mandated territories to national independence. Not endowed with gifts of historical prophecy with which to predict those developments, most of the colonial experts in 1919 thought it would be only a matter of time until the mandates became normal colonies. 'You will see', one of the French delegates said to Wilson's colonial advisor, 'what these mandates will develop into in ten years'.[10] Far from envisaging the eventual independence of colonies such as German East Africa, Allied statesmen at the Peace Conference regarded 1919 as the renewal, not the end, of an imperial era.

Historians have often puzzled over who was responsible for inventing the idea of mandates, and have usually identified General Smuts as the originator. In general that answer is correct. He more than any other statesman developed the idea of mandatory control—though it has not been brought out sufficiently that one of the main reasons he accepted mandates in tropical Africa was because he hoped that the Portuguese colonies also would be placed under international control,

[10] Typescript copy of George Louis Beer's Diary (Library of Congress), 7–13 July 1919.

thereby giving Britain a pretext for intervention, if necessary, in Portuguese Africa. Did Smuts and his colleagues have any particular precedent for the mandates system in mind? Historians have speculated that, among other things, the idea of mandates descended from the traditions of the Roman Empire, sixteenth century Spanish political theory, and Burke's dictum that the nature of a trust is accountability. Those in the British Government did not search for such remote origins. According to the Colonial Secretary at the time of the Peace Conference, Lord Milner, the British administration of Egypt seemed especially relevant:

Lord Milner pointed out that the mandatory principle was not altogether an innovation. Our administration of Egypt for thirty-five years was carried on on that principle, and subject to innumerable obligations which we consistently fulfilled, at one time to the extent of giving a decided preference to other nations over ourselves.[11]

In the opinion however of Lord Reading, Ambassador in the United States, 'giving Egypt as an example might not altogether appeal either to France or America'.[12] Perhaps for that reason Egypt as an 'antecedent' of the mandates system received less attention than two other African examples, the Congo and, to a lesser extent, Morocco. The Prime Minister thought that the Berlin Act of 1885, which established international control over the conventional basin of the Congo, embodied the idea of trusteeship. According to him, there was 'no large difference between the mandatory principle and the principles laid down by the Berlin Conference'.[13] A good case could be made that he was not entirely wrong. The basic principle of both was free trade (not even applied to the 'C' mandates of South-West Africa and the Pacific islands, thus making the free-trade zone in tropical Africa only slightly larger than the one of the Berlin Act), which, according to the nineteenth century formula, would promote the peaceful development of colonial territories to the benefit of the native inhabitants and Europeans alike. Both the Berlin Act and the mandates system embodied unsuccessful attempts at neutralization in the event of war. The Japanese ignored the clauses

[11] Imperial War Cabinet Minutes, Secret, 20 Dec. 1918, CAB. 23/40.
[12] *Ibid.* For other analogies see C.O. memorandum of 27 Jan. 1919, C.O. 537/1020.
[13] *Foreign Relations, Paris Peace Conference,* III, p. 750.

designed to prevent fortification of the islands, just as over twenty years earlier the powers with the most to gain by conducting military operations in colonial territories ignored the German effort to invoke the optional neutrality clause of the Berlin Act. Sir Eyre Crowe of the Foreign Office in the early days of the war explained why Britain refused to consider restricting the war to the European theatre: 'neutralization-plans are a futile absurdity. What is wanted is to strike hard with all our might in all the four corners of the world'.[14]

British colonial aims were constant throughout the war. The main goal was to absorb the German colonies in the vicinity of the southern Dominions of South Africa, Australia and New Zealand: South-West Africa and the German islands south of the Equator. Next in priority came German East Africa, which formed the 'missing link' in the chain of British possessions stretching from South Africa to Egypt. As in the days of the partition of Africa, British statesmen attached more strategic importance to the eastern part of the continent than to the western. They yielded most of the Cameroons and Togoland to France. Uppermost in their minds as they pondered the future of these territories was the determination not to see any of them returned to Germany—a guarantee eventually secured by Article 119 of the Treaty of Versailles, which deprived Germany of her colonial empire. Moral as well as strategic considerations shaped British policy in this regard. As Professor Stengers has recently written, 'In August 1914, the Germans became the Huns. The moral shock provoked in England by the German aggression—a shock of extraordinary magnitude— was the major factor which governed all later developments. . . . The Germans lost their colonies on the fields of Liège and in the blackened ruins of Louvain. Huns could not be entrusted with the sacred task of civilizing other peoples'[15]—nor could they be permitted to hold strategic positions around the globe. According to a South African newspaper, the *Cape Times*, in 1918: 'There is no clash in the question of the future settlement of the German colonies between the expedient and the morally right. Both the signposts point in the same direction'.[16]

[14] Minute by Crowe, (37507), 10 Aug. 1914, F.O. 371/2016. See especially Jonathan E. Helmreich, 'The End of Congo Neutrality, 1914', *Historian*, XXVIII (Aug. 1966).
[15] In *Imperial Rivalry and Colonial Rule*.　　[16] 29 Aug. 1918.

In the minds of most Englishmen, there was no contradiction
in the proposition that the acquisition of most of the German
colonies was necessary for the welfare of the inhabitants as well
as for the security of the Empire. To South Africans and Australasians, the main justification for keeping the colonies was the
protection of their frontiers from German aggression in the
future. In England, humanitarians emphasized German atrocities in the colonies. Within the Government, Lord Curzon
probably gave the most common answer to the question of why
Britain should extend British rule over the German colonies
when he asked rhetorically, 'why should England do this? Why
should Great Britain push herself out in these directions? Of
course, the answer is obvious—India'.[17]

*   *   *

There were two groups of German colonies, the ones in the
Pacific and the Far East, and the ones in Africa. The colonial
empire was over 1,000,000 square miles, almost five times
larger than the mother country. The European population in
the colonies was small: at the outbreak of the war, approximately 25,000, of whom about 20,000 were Germans. Most of
the European emigration to the colonies took place in the early
years, and by 1913 only about 30 Germans a year went to
settle permanently—approximately one out of 1,000 annual
German emigrants. Germany's trade with the colonies amounted
to only 0·6 per cent. of her total exports and 0·5 per cent. of her
total imports. The overseas Empire never ran at a profit; in
1913 the deficit amounted to over £6,000,000. But the value
of the colonies cannot be measured statistically, if only because
of the popular belief that great nations possessed colonial empires.
The statistics below are for 1914 or shortly before:

FAR EAST AND PACIFIC

Kiaochow. 193 square miles, 84,000 Chinese population,
approximately 1,700 German civilians and a garrison of about
2,400 military personnel. Legend has it that at the beginning
of the war the only airplane in Kiaochow, 'das Flugzeug von
Tsingtau', somehow managed to fly back to Germany. The

---

[17] Eastern Committee Minutes, Secret, 9 Dec. 1918, CAB. 27/24.

seizure of this foothold in the Shantung peninsula in 1897 was perhaps the most dramatic of Germany's colonial ventures, and gave her a voice in the Far East she had not previously possessed. To some it seemed to foreshadow the eventual partition of China. For the same reason the British watched suspiciously the Japanese takeover of Kiaochow and the 21 Demands on China. The Anglo-Japanese Alliance was an uneasy one. In the words of Lord Robert Cecil of the Foreign Office, 'The commercial as well as the military & perhaps the political methods of Japan appear to be founded on those of Germany'.[18] The British feared the advent of Japan as a 'Pan-Asiatic' power, which, apart from adversely affecting British influence in the Far East, might cause 'an increase of native unrest . . . in India'.[19]

Islands North of the Equator. These Islands consisted of three main groups, the Carolines and Palau (Pelew) islands, 550 square miles, native population about 40,000; the Marianas (Ladrones), 241 square miles, native population 3,000; and the Marshalls, 176 square miles, native population about 11,000. The European population of the Carolines and Marianas (purchased from Spain in 1898–99) was very slight, probably less than 150. In the Marshalls (acquired in 1885) there were about 180 Europeans, of whom 76 were Germans. All of these islands were seized by the Japanese. Many are mere coral reefs enclosing lagoons. The British Admiralty guessed during the war that only seven of them possessed harbours. So little did the British know of the political geography of this part of the Pacific that they requested the Australian task force to proceed to Yap in the Carolines in the belief that it was the seat of government. In fact the administrative center was Jaluit in the Marshall group, but Yap did possess an important wireless station.

Islands South of the Equator. Samoa, 1,000 square miles, 33,550 native population, about 550 Europeans, of whom 330 were German and 140 British. After long imperial rivalry the Samoan islands were finally partitioned in 1899 between the United States and Germany. Britain in return received the Tonga islands, which form the larger part of the Solomon group. Robert Louis Stevenson convalesced in Samoa and

[18] Minute by Cecil, c. 9 May 1916 (83294), F.O. 371/2693.
[19] India Office memorandum, c. 16 May 1916, F.O. 371/2693.

described the rivalry between the powers in *A Footnote to History* (London, 1892). Shortly after German Samoa fell before New Zealand troops in August 1914, the *Daily Telegraph* commented that he 'would have rejoiced, had he lived, to see the occupation of Samoa by British [troops]. Everyone who has read his . . . [book] is well aware that the German administration there has been an exceedingly bad one'.

Bismarck Archipelago. 20,000 square miles. Native population 260,000, white population about 820. Nauru, an island beyond the archipelago, but south of the Equator, was of considerable economic value because of phosphate deposits. It consequently caused a squabble in the British Empire Delegation at the Peace Conference as to who should become the mandatory power. The mandate was eventually conferred on Australia on behalf of the British Empire, while New Zealand received Samoa and Australia all the other German islands south of the Equator.

Kaiser Wilhelmsland (northeastern New Guinea). 93,000 square miles. Native population estimated anywhere between 550,000 and 750,000. White population about 970. New Guinea, which the Germans annexed despite the strong protest of the Queensland government in Australia, was the largest German territory in the Pacific. Its seat of government was at Rabaul in the Bismarck Archipelago. New Guinea contained the most primitive population of any of the German colonies. When President Wilson at the Peace Conference asked whether American missionaries would be prevented entry to New Guinea if Australia became the mandatory power, Prime Minister Hughes reputedly said, 'Certainly not, Mr. President, I understand that these poor people often go for months at a time without enough to eat'.

AFRICAN COLONIES

South-West Africa. 322,200 square miles. Native population around 80,000, Europeans under 15,000. The chief centres of European population were Windhoek, the capital of the interior; Swakopmund, the principal port; and Lüderitz Bay. South-West Africa was the first German colony. During the war Curzon referred bitterly to 'The weakness and procrastination of the British Government in the early 'eighties that impelled

Bismarck to the annexation of this territory by Germany.'[20] Mainly desert, the colony was nevertheless one of the few places where white settlers could live permanently as farmers and ranchers in a German overseas territory. It also possessed mineral wealth. In 1904 General von Trotha brutally suppressed the uprising of the Hereros, an event that caused much more indignation in England during the First World War than at the time. Some South Africans of Boer stock always regarded South-West Africa, in Smut's words, as 'part of our Afrikaner heritage'.[21] After the Second World War the South African Government refused to place the territory under the control of the Trusteeship Council of the United Nations, contending that the mandate had lapsed with the demise of the League. Ethiopia and Liberia, as the only two former African members of the League, in 1960 brought suit against South Africa before the International Court of Justice for having violated the 'sacred trust' of the mandate. On 19 July 1966 the Court threw out the case on the grounds of a technicality, but on 27 October of the same year the General Assembly of the United Nations proclaimed the termination of the mandate.

Togoland. 34,000 square miles, about half the size of Oklahoma. Native population over 1,000,000. 360 Europeans, of whom 320 were Germans. Togoland was Germany's smallest colony, but nevertheless a 'model' because it was the only one that was self-sufficient. The administrative center was Lomé. Apparently the first British shots of the First World War were fired in Togoland—the only remarkable feature of the territory's history during the war.

Cameroons. 190,000 square miles (after the 1911 Moroccan agreement, 292,000 square miles). About one and a half times the size of Germany. Native population over 2,650,000. 1,871 Europeans, of whom 1,643 were Germans. Duala, the capital, is one of the best ports on the west coast, which the British belatedly tried to annex in 1884, but to which at the time they attached little strategic significance. During the war the

[20] Memorandum by Curzon, Secret, G.-182, 'German and Turkish Territories Captured in the War', 5 Dec. 1917, CAB. 24/4.
[21] Smuts to D. Reitz, 22 Sept. 1914, quoted by Sir Keith Hancock and Dr. Jean van der Poel in *Selections from the Smuts Papers* (4 vols., Cambridge, 1966), III, p. 198. I am indebted to Dr. van der Poel for allowing me to read this work in page-proof.

Cameroons formed the main African bone of contention between the British and French. One Colonial Office official noted
the irony of this: 'It is a curious thing that we looked with indifference on the occupation of Duala by our declared enemy,
but are up in arms at the idea of its passing to our ally'.[22]
In 1911, as a result of the Moroccan crisis, Germany enlarged
the frontiers of the colony by acquiring from France two strips
of territory (they reverted to France in full sovereignty at the
Peace Conference) that pointed like 'daggers' towards the
Belgian Congo—thus to British eyes symbolising German
dreams of a *Mittelafrika*. Economically the Cameroons had the
most potential for development, and, if linked with the Congo,
theoretically might have enabled Germany to exploit the heart
of the continent for militaristic purposes. Sir Eyre Crowe of the
Foreign Office summed up what he believed to be the reasons
why Germany wanted a central African empire when he wrote:
'The value is great from a military and strategical, as well as
from an economic point of view (supply of copper, rubber,
oil &c. &c.)'.[23]

German East Africa. 384,000 square miles. Total native population about 7,500,000, of which 3,500,000 were concentrated in
the northwestern districts of Ruanda and Urundi. European
population, 5,336. German East Africa had perhaps the most
romantic aura of all of the German colonies and was conceived
of in some circles as becoming the equivalent of Britain's
Empire in India (a few Englishmen during the war transformed
this idea and speculated about German East Africa as a
'colony for India'). In the late 1880s the struggle for the
interior threatened to become an explosive issue between
Britain and Germany. Part of the trouble arose from the activities of one of the most bloodthirsty of all German imperialists,
Carl Peters, whom Hitler later called 'a model, if stern,
administrator'. The British press during the war recalled in
vivid detail Peters' atrocities of beating natives until their
backs were like 'chopped meat'. In 1890 the two countries
delimited their spheres of influence, the Germans relinquishing
ambitions of acquiring Uganda and the sources of the Nile, the
British placing the 'missing link' of the Cape to Cairo route in

[22] Minute by Fiddes, 1 Dec. 1914, C.O. 583/20.
[23] Minute by Crowe, 16 Dec. 1917 (228898), F.O. 371/2860.

German hands. One of the remarkable features of British colonial aims during the war was the fervour with which the great vision of the Cape to Cairo scheme was revived, in no small part by the explorer who had popularized the idea in the late 1880s, Sir Harry Johnston. The following extract from one of his letters, though exaggerated and in places inaccurate (especially the part about the Colonial Office, where exactly the opposite was true), indicates the emotional quality of the issue of German East Africa and the Cape to Cairo route, and is a good example of how many Englishmen felt about the German colonies in general: 'I . . . from the very outset of my African career was filled with the Cape-to-Cairo purpose. . . . What bee is in all your bonnets. The Colonial Office—damn it—already wants to give Ruanda to Belgium; that poisonous little organ of the Liverpool merchants, [E.D.] Morel's *West African Mail*, wants to give much of G.E.A. to Portugal. . . . Why? Why? Why? You none of you know G.E.A. I do. You none of you seem to consider for one moment the feelings of the natives of G.E.A. . . . The only point on which we agree is that NEVER AGAIN—— IF WE CONQUER——shall Germany rule in Africa or Asia'.[24]

[24] Johnston to Harris, 16 Sept. 1916, Harris Papers in possession of Lady Harris. Most of Sir John Harris's correspondence may be found in the papers of the Anti-Slavery and Aborigines Protection Society, Rhodes House, Oxford.

1. COOPERATION OR RIVALRY?
1884–1914

THE doctrine of Germany's guilt as a uniquely brutal and cruel colonial power originated during the First World War, not before. But the idea that German colonies were strategically valuable developed during the three decades after the beginning of the German colonial empire in 1884. The purpose of the following remarks is not to relate generally the history of Anglo-German relations before the war (which may be found in many other works), but to discuss specifically the development of British ideas about the strategic problem of the German colonies in Africa, and, to a lesser extent, in the Pacific. The reason for the African emphasis is this. In the decades before the war, the problems of the Pacific (apart from those of China) seemed remote to the Government in London and often insignificant; but issues at stake with Germany in Africa often touched upon the dual points of control over the route to India, Egypt and southern Africa. In Africa also lay the choice for British statesmen of whether to appease Germany by giving her a bigger 'place in the sun', usually at the expense of Belgium or Portugal; or whether to pursue the traditional British policy of supporting the empires of small, neutral or allied states as buffers in order to keep out a great European power—the same choice, in a different way, that faced Britain in regard to German *Weltpolitik* in the Middle and Far East.[1]

[1] In this chapter I have drawn on my essay in *Imperial Rivalry and Colonial Rule*. The bibliographical chapter of that work contains a very full discussion of both British and German sources for the 1884–1914 period. Some of the more important works are these. On the general question of the partition of Africa, see Ronald Robinson and John Gallagher with Alice Denny, *Africa and the Victorians* (London, 1961); and William L. Langer, *The Diplomacy of Imperialism* (New York, 1956 edn.). On imperial rivalry in West Africa, see John D. Hargreaves, *Prelude to the Partition of West Africa* (London, 1963); John E. Flint, *Sir George Goldie and the Making of Nigeria* (London, 1960); C. W. Newbury, *The Western Slave Coast and its Rulers* (Oxford, 1961); and Harry R. Rudin, *Germans in the Cameroons* (New Haven, 1938). On East Africa, F. F. Müller, *Deutschland-Zanzibar-Ostafrika* (East Berlin, 1959), and Roland Oliver, *Sir Harry Johnston and the Scramble for Africa* (London, 1957). On South Africa, J. S. Marais, *The Fall of Kruger's Republic* (London, 1961); and G. H. L. Le May, *British Supremacy in South Africa, 1899–1907* (Oxford,

Within a year from the summer of 1884 Germany acquired an overseas empire in Africa and the Pacific. By doing so the Germans violated the English maxim that there were three methods of colonization: 'the English, which consists in making colonies with colonists; the German, which collects colonists without colonies; and the French, which sets up colonies without colonists'.[2] The British response to this change in character of the German colonial movement varied greatly. On the whole the British press as well as the Government in 1884–85, though objecting to Bismarck's way of empire building, did not regard his schemes as a challenge to British commerce or power. Commercially, the British tended to see Germany as a free trading nation. Strategically, they recognized 'the comparatively insignificant naval power of the [German] Empire'.[3] If the Germans, despite their lack of 'colonial aptitude' were foolish enough to embark on ventures in places such as the 'sterile sand hole' of South-West Africa, Englishmen generally were willing to give 'a hearty welcome to the development of the Teuton abroad'.[4]

Strategy nevertheless did play an important role in British colonial deliberations of 1884–85. The Secretary of State for India, Lord Kimberley, feared that the French and the Germans with their 'aggressive spirit' might 'oust' Britain from the East African coast, thereby endangering India.[5] Sir Clement Hill of the Foreign Office urged that Britain should give way on the west coast of Africa in order to secure the east coast—'where the political future of the country is of real importance to Indian and imperial interests'.[6] So far as the west coast was concerned, the Foreign Office could state that the British Government had 'no jealousy of the Germans as neighbours in those territories [Togoland and the Cameroons]; they welcome them as friendly rivals in the race of commerce and civilization'. On the east coast those assurances were given much less willingly—for the same reason that lay behind Salisbury's Nile policy and, during

1965). On the Congo, R. T. Anstey, *Britain and the Congo in the Nineteenth Century* (Oxford, 1962). On the Pacific, J. M. Ward, *British Policy in the South Pacific, 1783–1893* (Sydney, 1948); and W. P. Morrell, *Britain in the Pacific Islands* (Oxford, 1960).

[2] *The Times*, 27 Aug. 1884.   [3] *Ibid.*, 25 June 1884.

[4] *Daily Telegraph*, 22 Oct. 1884.

[5] Kimberley to Granville, 21 Nov. and 21 Dec., 1884, P.R.O. 30/29/126, Granville Papers.

[6] Quoted in Robinson and Gallagher, *Africa and the Victorians*, p. 191.

the First World War, the Imperial War Cabinet's principle that guided British plans for the peace settlement: Britain's position in East Africa was vitally important for the defence of India.

The East African problem in turn was connected with that of South Africa. The head of the African Department of the Foreign Office, Sir Percy Anderson, feared that the Germans might develop trans-continental ambitions by buying the strategic port of Delagoa Bay from the Portuguese. 'If Germany were to get it she would at once be brought into the Transvaal and the head waters of the Orange river, and so might even stretch out a hand to the new [German] settlement in Angra Pequeña [in South-West Africa]'.[7] That possibility alarmed the Cape government even more than the one in London. So far as the South Africans were concerned, the Germans should never have been permitted to settle in South-West Africa in the first place. According to the Cape Town correspondent of the *Standard*, 'The general opinion here is that there is not room for two flags in South Africa'.[8] The same was true in the Pacific. From the Australasian point of view, the Germans should never have been given the chance to jeopardize British security there. 'The settlers [in Australia]', the Colonial Secretary, Lord Derby, wrote to Gladstone, '. . . cannot bear the notion of a German settlement on the north coast of New Guinea'.[9] In 1884–85 the British Government found itself in the dilemma of having to choose between supporting the demands of the South Africans and Australasians to block German expansion, or of appeasing Bismarck. Gladstone followed the latter course. As he described his 'old fashioned' notions about strategy to Derby: 'Is it dignified, or is it required by any real interest, to make extensions of British authority without any view of occupying but simply to keep them [the Germans] out?'[10] The permanent staff of the Foreign Office and Colonial Office would have phrased the proposition in a different way: cooperation with Germany at least had the merit of keeping out Britain's historic colonial rival, France.

[7] Minute by Anderson, 27 Oct. 1884, F.O. 84/1814.
[8] *Standard*, 27 Dec. 1884.
[9] Derby to Gladstone, Private, 23 Dec. 1884, Gladstone Papers, British Museum, Add. Mss. 44142.
[10] Gladstone to Derby (copy), 30 Dec. 1884, Gladstone Papers, Add. Mss. 44142.

Even in the early years of colonial relations between the two countries, British attitudes could be divided between those of regarding Anglo-German friendship as one of the keys to European peace, and those of suspecting a world-wide German conspiracy. In the first decade, 1884–94, the former view definitely predominated. The permanent officials at the Foreign Office, at least, saw in a vague way that Bismarck was manipulating the colonial question for reasons connected with German politics as well as European diplomacy, and that he was trying to secure markets overseas at a time when it seemed that Germany might eventually be excluded from the colonial world. But despite that awareness on the part of a few civil servants, the Foreign Secretary, Lord Granville, did not respond to Bismarck's overtures for British support—and the bureaucratic ineptitude of the Colonial Office in dealing with the question of South-West Africa strengthened Bismarck's suspicions that the British were trying to obstruct his colonial policy. Mutual misunderstanding outraged Bismarck and embittered those in the British Government. The Foreign Office, though willing to recognize Germany's annexations as 'accomplished facts—with a complaint as to the manner'[11]—believed Bismarck had been less than frank about his intentions and was guilty of sharp practice. That indignation may be traced through the British reaction to each of Germany's major colonial acquisitions.

The Cameroons, July, 1884: 'the unfair and unfriendly manner in which Germany had acted in the Cameroons'.[12] South-West Africa, August 1884: 'Germany has behaved badly to us'.[13] New Guinea, December 1884: '... I [Joseph Chamberlain] am not afraid of German colonisation, but I don't like to be cheeked by Bismarck or anyone else'.[14] German East Africa, May 1885: 'the excessive impatience of the Chancellor and his inclination to high-handed proceedings'.[15] Only in regard to Togoland did the British respond with relative indifference. According to an Admiralty official, 'the eventual

---

[11] Granville to Malet, Private, 23 Dec. 1884, F.O. 343/2, Malet Papers.
[12] Minute by T. V. Lister, 4 Dec. 1884, F.O. 84/1660.
[13] Minute by Herbert (14068), 19 Aug. 1884, C.O. 417/1.
[14] Quoted in J. L. Garvin, *Joseph Chamberlain* (3 vols., 1932–34), I, p. 497.
[15] Malet to Granville, 20 June 1885, quoted in Paul Knaplund, ed., *Letters from the Berlin Embassy* (Washington, 1944), pp. 413–14.

collision with [French] Dahomey will most likely fall to the lot of Germany instead of England'.[16] Those attitudes left their mark on those who shaped British policy in the decade before the First World War. Over twenty years after the founding of Germany's colonial empire, one of the arch-Germanophobes of the Foreign Office, Sir Eyre Crowe, wrote that it was 'difficult to find a better word than "deception" ' for Bismarck's action.[17] The most historically minded member of the War Cabinet during the war, Lord Curzon, pointed to what he believed to be the moral of the story when he condemned the feeble policy of the British Government in the 1880s.[18] A strong British Government, according to Curzon's school of thought, would have stood up to Bismarck, prevented Germany from acquiring colonies, and would have thus prevented Anglo-German colonial rivalry from becoming a cause of the war.

British statesmen in the 1880s did not regard the German colonial movement as a necessary irritant in the relations between the two countries, still less as a possible cause of war. They saw France, not Germany, as the great threat to British commerce and security. The aim was Anglo-German cooperation in colonial affairs to secure free trade and to block French expansion —a goal achieved at the Berlin Conference of 1884–85 despite Franco-German efforts to work against Britain.[19] Lord Granville simply acquiesced, but at the same time made it clear that the free trade policy of Britain was more compatible with Germany's interests than the protectionist policy of France.

When Lord Salisbury returned to the Foreign Office in June 1885 the only serious colonial question between the two countries was that of Zanzibar. His attitude towards that issue was shaped by his desire to align Britain with Germany on European issues. 'Our policy', he once wrote, 'is identical with that of the Central Powers. England and Germany and to a great extent Austria

[16] Memorandum by Sir F. Richard, 4 Dec. 1884, enclosed in Northbrook to Granville, Private, 20 Dec. 1884, P.R.O. 30/29/140, Granville Papers.
[17] G. P. Gooch and Harold Temperley, eds., *British Documents on the Origins of the War*, III, pp. 397–431.
[18] Memorandum by Curzon, Secret, G.-182, 'German and Turkish Territories Captured in the War', 5 Dec. 1917, CAB. 24/4.
[19] On this point see especially S. E. Crowe, *The Berlin West African Conference* (London, 1942), *passim*.

are "satisfied" Powers. France and Russia are "hungry" Powers'.[20] Applying that principle to East Africa, Salisbury at first regarded Bismarck's colonial schemes as little more than a passing aberration. He rightly believed Bismarck's true aim was financial profit for German businessmen, not colonial expansion by the German Government. If a war between Germany and Spain were to break out, Salisbury commented in September 1885, 'I suppose Bismarck will take the Philippines, which will ... be much more profitable than any part of Africa'.[21] Salisbury's policy at this stage consisted of buying German friendship by giving way on colonial questions.

The great test of Salisbury's 'collaboration' policy came at the close of the 1880s in East Africa. There his tolerant attitude towards the 'unwise display of swagger of the Germans' did not produce all of the results he hoped for. The German East Africa Company did not, as the Foreign Office vainly wished, 'collapse without attracting much attention'.[22] Instead the British were confronted with a full-scale German race for the interior led by Carl Peters, who pressed inland towards the great lakes and Uganda making treaties and raising German flags. By the winter of 1889 the Germans threatened to destroy the basis of British African policy by securing the sources of the Nile, which Salisbury and the Foreign Office believed to be essential for the defence of Egypt and the route to India. The next spring Salisbury's difficulties were compounded by the fall of Bismarck. Whatever Salisbury may have felt about Bismarck's methods, he knew that the German Chancellor could be relied upon to subordinate African questions to European ones. Faced with the uncertainty of German policy after Bismarck's fall, and with the explosive issue of the East African hinterland, Salisbury decided that the time had come to reach a settlement. Fortunately from the British point of view, Bismarck's successor, Caprivi, and the Foreign Secretary, Marschall, also desired to curtail colonial

[20] 'Italy, it is true, is eminently a hungry Power; but the objects of her appetite are no great matter to us'. Salisbury to Sir Robert Morier, Private (copy), 1 Feb. 1888, Morier Papers, copies in possession of Miss Agatha Ramm, Somerville College, Oxford.
[21] Salisbury to Malet, Private (copy), 8 Sept. 1885, Salisbury Papers, Christ Church, Oxford.
[22] Minute by Anderson, 10 Mar. 1885, on Malet to Granville, No. 155 Africa, 5 Mar. 1885, F.O. 84/1713.

rivalry between the two countries. They wanted good relations with England, not an extensive African Empire, and were willing to compromise on almost all points.

In the negotiations that led to the Anglo-German agreement on 1 July 1890, Salisbury yielded on only one important issue: he acquiesced in the German demand to have land communication between German East Africa and the Congo, thus breaking a possible chain of British territories from South Africa to Egypt. Though there was an outcry from the Chartered Companies in East and South Africa, Salisbury brushed aside criticism on this point by referring to the Cape to Cairo scheme as a 'curious idea' and by mocking the notion that a thin, connecting strip of territory could ever be commercially or strategically valuable. He reached agreement with the Germans on the main points at issue by ceding Heligoland, an island in the North Sea that had been retained by the British after the Napoleonic wars. For reasons of prestige and naval strategy, the Germans eagerly accepted and did not place difficulties in the way of reaching agreement about various disputes in Africa. The colonial settlement of 1890 was overwhelmingly favourable to the British and a great triumph for Salisbury. As Sir John Kirk, the former British Consul in Zanzibar, summed it up, 'the Anglo-German Agreement secur[es] . . . to us Uganda and a free hand in a good square block with an open road to the Nile . . .'.[23] Nevertheless Salisbury's diplomacy was critically regarded by the men in power during the First World War. As Lord Curzon asked in 1917: 'Did the late Lord Salisbury by ceding Heligoland to Germany in Europe, or by yielding to her Dar-es-Salaam and the hinterland opposite Zanzibar in Africa, and deflecting the frontier line at every point to her advantage and our own detriment, conciliate her good will? This war supplies the answer'.[24]

In England the 1890 agreement was interpreted as Germany's decision not to become a great African power, and not to challenge Britain for colonial supremacy. Despite the continued

[23] Kirk to Lugard, 18 July 1890, Lugard Papers, Rhodes House, Oxford.
[24] The same document cited in note 18. Salisbury had no way of knowing, of course, that during the war Heligoland would be used as a submarine base. After the war the British seriously considered 'blowing up or otherwise destroying the Island'. A. J. Balfour, 'Notes on Heligoland' (copy), 14 Apr. 1919, Lothian (Philip Kerr) Papers, Scottish Record Office.

friction in the Pacific over Samoa, colonial rivalry between the two countries seemed curtailed. The 1890 settlement eliminated Germany as a competitor for the great imperial goal of the late nineteenth century, control of the sources of the Nile. Nevertheless the Germans continued to play an important role in the rivalry between the British and the French for that strategic region. Having closed the gate to the Nile in the south, the Foreign Office now attempted to enlist German support in blocking the French advance in the west. The Germans had good reason to cooperate since they feared French encroachment in the northern Cameroons. In 1893 Britain and Germany concluded another agreement, by which the two countries delimited their spheres in West Africa up to Lake Chad. It merely meant a division of the spoils before the arrival of the French. The Germans gained a favourable settlement in the hinterland; the British, theoretically at least, blockaded the road to the Nile against the French. But from the British point of view the success was short lived. In March 1894 the French cut through the British paper barricade by concluding their own agreement with the Germans. It cleared the way for the French penetration of the Nile valley as well as for further French advances in the Niger basin. The German collaboration with French plans— at a time when the system of alliances was also shifting in Europe —had momentous consequences for the colonial relations between Britain and Germany. The British believed that they had been double-crossed. The era of Anglo-German colonial friendship had come to a close.

The second decade of Anglo-German colonial relations opened on an ominous note of violent German reaction to the Congo agreement of 1894. In the spring of that year Britain concluded an arrangement with the Congo State designed to block France's advance to the Nile. When published, the agreement created a sensation. The French learned that the Congo State had been shoved in as a buffer between them and the Nile; while the Germans saw with astonishment that German East Africa had been 'encircled' by the Cape to Cairo route running along the eastern boundary of the Congo State. The Cape to Cairo clause in the agreement was a colossal blunder. The Foreign Office demanded its inclusion at the last moment merely as a *quid pro quo* for one of King Leopold's demands. Apparently Sir Percy Anderson

thought merely in terms of communication between Uganda
and Lake Tanganyika, without recognizing that he was raising
the Cape to Cairo bogey. Because of the 'corridor' clause,
Germany as well as France protested against the agreement.
As in 1884, Britain found the two major western colonial powers
aligned against her. Commentaries appeared in the press that
France might reconvene the Berlin Conference and perhaps
even partition the Congo State. In view of these alarming possi-
bilities, the Foreign Office chose to cancel the corridor clause.
The crisis demonstrated the truth of the 'favourite axiom' of the
Director of the colonial division of the German Foreign Office,
Dr. Paul Kayser: 'that there are but three powers in Africa,
England, France and Germany, two of which must inevitably
combine against the third'.[25]

Despite the 'violence'[26] displayed by the Germans in 1894,
and despite the implicit threat of blackmail in Kayser's 'axiom',
the British continued to try to work in concert with the Germans.
They recognized that both governments had one overriding
colonial concern in common: to prevent France from becoming,
in Kayser's words, 'the mistress of Africa'. The Germans themselves wished to cooperate by partitioning the Portuguese colonies between Britain and Germany and by making a far reaching
agreement that would resolve all outstanding colonial disputes
such as those in Samoa and the hinterland of Togoland. Kayser
'felt convinced that Portugal could not for long hold her own in
South-East Africa'. According to a British memorandum
recording his views:

"Why", Dr. Kayser said, "cannot all these matters be settled by
another Anglo-German Agreement? We shall be quite ready to
come into conference with maps and rulers and pencils, if it were
possible to settle the bases of an agreement beforehand. . . . I feel
sure it would be in the interest of the good relations of both parties,

[25] As recounted in Gosselin's memorandum of 30 Aug. 1894, F.O.
64/1334. Kimberley, the Colonial Secretary, wrote in this connection: 'We
are not likely, it seems, to have less difficulty with the Germans than the
French. Both are equally jealous of us, & will do all they can to thwart us
in Africa'. Minute by Kimberley, 4 Sept., on Gosselin to Kimberley, No.
96 Africa, 31 Aug. 1894, F.O. 64/1334.
[26] Anderson wrote that there was 'absolutely no argument' in the
German position. 'It is simply violence'. Minute by Anderson on Malet to
Kimberley, No. 12 Africa tel., 15 June 1894, F.O. 64/1335.

were all these causes of misunderstanding and colonial jealousies once for all removed'.[27]

When Salisbury was returned to office after the fall of the Liberal Government in June 1895, 'colonial jealousy' between the two countries continued to be one of his main concerns. Despite the changing balance of power in the Far East brought about by Germany's seizure of Kiaochow in 1897, African questions, as in the previous decade, were the main point of colonial friction between the two countries.[28] In the last years of the nineteenth century, the problem of southern Africa, above all, exacerbated Anglo-German relations. Salisbury wanted to continue his collaboration policy: 'We certainly wish to be good friends with Germany: as good friends as we were in 1892. That is to say, we wish to lean to the Triple Alliance without belonging to it'.[29] But he resented schemes such as the one propounded by Kayser because he felt that Germans had no business intervening in southern Africa. 'Of course Germany has no rights in the affair', he once wrote about the Transvaal.[30] The British were galled at Germany's 'coquetting' with the Transvaal and meddling with its gateway, the Portuguese port of Delagoa Bay. So strongly did the British Ambassador in Berlin feel about this point that he concluded his career in October 1895 by telling the German Foreign Secretary that there would be 'War' between the two countries if Germany continued to interfere.

Two months later the Kaiser sent his congratulations to President Kruger of the Transvaal. During the First World War *The Times* remembered the Kruger telegram as the event which 'first revealed' all of the 'long intrigue' against the British people.[31] At the time the British public reacted explosively. According to one commentator, one of the main reasons was colonial:

[27] Quoted in Gosselin's memorandum of 1 Dec. 1894, encl. in Malet to Kimberley, No. 150 Africa Confidential, F.O. 64/1334.

[28] For the other main problem in Anglo-German relations at this time, naval rivalry, see especially Jonathan Steinberg, *Yesterday's Deterrent: Tirpitz and the Birth of the German Battle Fleet* (London, 1965).

[29] Salisbury to Lascelles, Private (copy), 10 Mar. 1896, Salisbury Papers.

[30] Salisbury to Chamberlain, Private, 30 Dec. 1895, Joseph Chamberlain Papers, Birmingham University Library.

[31] 10 July 1915.

The sensitive point is this, that the expansion of Germany is barred in Europe, and that out of Europe Germany encounters England everywhere. . . .

The real and deep-seated object of the German Colonial party is to find some part of the world where Germans can emigrate to and live as Germans. They look on South Africa, if ruled by the Dutch elements, as such a place. . . . [32]

Whatever ambitions German colonial jingoes may have had regarding the Transvaal, the Kaiser himself was willing to be squared—a political fact that led Joseph Chamberlain (Colonial Secretary, 1895–1903), to remark in 1899 that German policy since Bismarck had been 'one of undisguised blackmail'.[33] In return 'for their abandonment of the Boers & the Transvaal', the Germans demanded a prospective share of the Portuguese colonies. 'They are not content to wait for events to give them their share of Portuguese territory', Salisbury wrote, 'but wish to force the pace of destiny'.[34] The Germans themselves did not regard these proceedings as extortion, but as 'the inauguration of a common Colonial Policy'.[35] After complicated negotiations, the British and the Germans agreed simply not to go into certain areas if the Portuguese Empire collapsed. Salisbury insisted on self-denying wording to render his real aim of buoying up the Portuguese colonies still possible. Should Portugal have to relinquish sovereignty, the property rights to her colonies would fall simultaneously to Britain and Germany. In that event Britain (according to the Agreement dated 30 August 1898) would receive southern Mozambique and central Angola;

[32] Cecil Spring Rice to Villiers, 17 Jan. and 21 Mar. 1896, F.O. 800/23; cf. Stephen Gwynn, ed., *The Letters and Friendships of Sir Cecil Spring Rice* (2 vols., Boston, 1929), I, pp. 191–92 and 201.

[33] Chamberlain to Salisbury, 18 Sept. 1899, Salisbury Papers. See Garvin, *Chamberlain*, III, pp. 307–30.

[34] Minute by Salisbury on Balfour to Lascelles, No. 153 Africa Confidential, 1 Sept. 1898, *British Documents*, I, p. 76.

[35] Bertie's memorandum of 19 Aug. 1898, Chamberlain Papers. For the German side see Fritz Schwarze, *Das Deutsch-Englische Abkommen über die Portugiesischen Kolonien vom 30 August 1898* (Göttingen, 1931); also (for German financial schemes in southern Angola) Horst Drechsler, 'Germany and S. Angola, 1898–1903', *Congresso Internacional de História dos Descobrimentos: Actas* (Lisbon, 1961), VI, pp. 73–89. The most illuminating British account of these Anglo-German negotiations and the alliance problems at the turn of the century is by J. A. S. Grenville, *Lord Salisbury and Foreign Policy* (London, 1964), chap. VIII.

Germany would get northern Mozambique and northern and southern Angola. For the British this bargain had several advantages. It divided the spoils before the arrival of the French (at a time when the two countries were already dangerously close to war at Fashoda); it meant the abandonment of the Transvaal by the Germans; and it strengthened the British hold over Delagoa Bay, without which they feared it would be difficult to conquer the Boers.

A few days after the outbreak of the Boer War the British pledged to defend the territorial integrity of the Portuguese Empire in return for Portuguese support. Though opportunistic, there was nothing inconsistent about this. The upholding of a minor power and an ally fitted perfectly into Salisbury's general policy. If the Portuguese Empire did disintegrate, the British would, as Chamberlain put it, 'be able to take care of ourselves in the scramble which would ensue'.[36] Salisbury prepared for that contingency by the Anglo-German Agreement; he then turned to Britain's ancient ally, Portugal, at a time when Portuguese assistance at Delagoa Bay was vitally needed. His demands of the Portuguese amounted practically to an ultimatum; but in return he promised to defend the Portuguese colonies—a guarantee, in Salisbury's mind, not contradictory with the Anglo-German Agreement. As it turned out, the Portuguese Empire did not collapse and the Anglo-German arrangement did not come into force. But the idea that it would whetted German appetites; and it demonstrated, to the British at least, that these appetites were, in Chamberlain's phrase, 'greedy'.[37] Because of the South African crisis the British submitted to German 'blackmail'—and not only in southern Africa. In the Pacific Salisbury acquiesced in the Samoan agreement of 1899 (which divided the group of islands between the United States and Germany, Britain receiving compensation in the Solomon group) and, a year earlier, had not protested against Germany's purchase of the Marianas, Carolines and other minor groups from Spain. The British at this time attached no strategic importance to the islands north

[36] Chamberlain to Salisbury, 15 Jan. 1899, Salisbury Papers.

[37] Robinson and Gallagher, *Africa and the Victorians*, p. 448. See also for this and other problems (especially those concerning relations in the Far East and more general problems of Anglo-German relations at the turn of the century) Grenville, *Lord Salisbury and Foreign Policy*.

of the Equator; but they uneasily watched Germany's acquisition of them because it seemed to provide even more evidence of a growing colonial appetite. As the Permanent Under-Secretary, Sir Thomas Sanderson, summed up the state of Anglo-German colonial relations at the turn of the century: 'To preserve German favour we are to pay and give way everywhere'.[38]

As the Berlin to Baghdad railway negotiations developed along with increasing commercial rivalry with Germany and friendlier relations with Russia, Englishmen tended more and more to see German schemes in the Middle East as a danger to the Empire. Lord Curzon reflected in 1918: 'The Baghdad Railway was a weapon directed at the heart of India'.[39] But at the turn of the century German schemes in the Middle East seemed much more chimerical than during the First World War. The real problem preoccupying the Foreign Office at this time was Germany's attitude towards the Boer War, which poisoned the lingering atmosphere of good will between the two countries. The German press vented its indignation at what it considered the ruthless way in which Britain was swallowing up two small, heroic republics; the British press responded (in the words of the Kaiser's commentary on *The Times*) with 'arrant lies' and 'fresh venom'. The 'odious accusations' of the Germans, according to Lord Lansdowne (Foreign Secretary, 1900–05) played an important part in the growing estrangement between Germany and Britain and in the shaping of the Anglo-French Entente of 1904. Colonial questions between Britain and Germany had little or nothing to do with that diplomatic revolution. Apart from South Africa, Anglo-German colonial issues at this time were minor ones—mostly West African boundary questions, towards which the British took a conciliatory attitude. By contrast, major territorial issues still confronted Britain in relation to France and Russia. They were resolved by the Anglo-French Entente of 1904 and the Anglo-Russian Entente of 1907. The former arrangement removed long standing grievances between France and Britain, notably those of Egypt and Morocco, while the latter agreement of 1907 attempted to settle the Persian and

---

[38] Minute by Sanderson on memorandum by Hill, 11 Feb. 1899, F.O. 2/223.
[39] 'We have destroyed it, and we do not mean to let it start again'. Eastern Committee Minues, Secret, 18 Dec. 1918, CAB. 27/24.

other questions. The Anglo-French Entente was not necessarily, at least in Lansdowne's view, directed against Germany. According to him the 'test case' as far as Germany was concerned would be Egypt. 'Will she [Germany] put a spoke in our wheel and stand out for all her privileges even if France, which has an infinitely larger stake in Egypt, consents to abdicate hers?' It would also be 'interesting', he wrote in 1904, to see how Germany would respond to France having a free hand in Morocco.[40]

A year later, the Germans demonstrated against the Moroccan clauses in the agreement. In March 1905 the Kaiser visited Tangier, indicating that Germany had no intention of relinquishing her rights in Morocco. But, according to Lansdowne, the agreements relating to the Entente, though dealing only with French and British affairs, provided 'adequate security for their [German] interests by maintaining the policy of the "open door" and equality of treatment, and the integrity of Morocco itself. What else does the Emperor want. . . ?'[41] The answer, Lansdowne surmised, was that the Germans wanted to drive a wedge into the Entente. If so, the attempt failed. Lansdowne's successor, Sir Edward Grey (Foreign Secretary, December 1905 –December 1916), was determined to stand by France. At the Conference of Algeciras, summoned in January 1906 to resolve the Moroccan crisis, Germany found herself driven into a corner, abandoned by all but Austria. After wringing a few concessions from France, Germany along with the other powers signed the Algeciras Act of 1906. This act secured the open door and provided for an international bank and a Franco–Spanish police force. A decade later the American publicist Walter Lippmann wrote that it was 'the most hopeful effort at world organization made up to the present'.[42] Along with the Berlin Act of 1885 the Algeciras Act became an important precedent for the establishment of the mandates system in 1919. This idealism of the First World War would have come as a surprise to the permanent officials of the British Foreign Office of 1906. They regarded the Algeciras Conference and its work merely

[40] Lansdowne to Lascelles (copy), 23 Mar. 1904, F.O. 800/128, Lansdowne Papers. The most recent, perceptive scholarship on the Entente negotiations is by George Monger, *The End of Isolation* (London, 1963).
[41] Lansdowne to Lascelles (copy), 9 Apr. 1905, F.O. 800/129.
[42] Walter Lippmann, *The Stakes of Diplomacy* (New York, 1915), p. 149.

as the result of Germany's attempt to exploit still another and even more dangerous colonial issue.

The permanent officials (such as Sir Charles Hardinge) clustered around Sir Edward Grey differed from those of a decade earlier (such as Sir Percy Anderson) by fearing the ambitions of Germany more than those of France—above all in Europe but also in Africa, the Middle East and Asia. Grey himself was moderate—willing to study 'the map of Africa . . . in a pro-German spirit'.[43] But, whenever he considered specific proposals such as whether to cede Walfisch Bay (the British possession off the coast of South-West Africa), he found himself checked by the strong opinions of his permanent officials, notably Hardinge, Sir Eyre Crowe, and Sir Francis Bertie. In regard to Walfisch Bay Hardinge wrote in 1907:

The possession of Walfish [sic] Bay by Germany would greatly facilitate any operations that they might intend against us in S. Africa. If Germany had possessed that port during the Boer War we should have had as much difficulty as at Delagoa Bay.[44]

Yet British possession of Walfisch Bay was a bone stuck in the German throat. '. . . The German Government realizes the fact that, in retaining Walfish [sic] Bay, the British have kept what is practically the key of the Protectorate'.[45] Grey recogniz-ed that the cession of the Bay would be impossible because of anti-German feeling at the Cape, but:

It seems to me that from the Imperial point of view it would be pushing things rather far for us to object to giving the Germans facilities at Walfisch Bay. . . . To object to everything uncondition-ally simply because it makes the Germans spend money at Swakop-mund [the port in South-West Africa] would be so churlish a policy that it would justify them in saying that we were really unfriendly and that their efforts to build a fleet against us must be increased.[46]

[43] Grey to Goschen, Private (copy), 29 Dec. 1911, F.O. 800/61, Grey Papers.

[44] Minute by Hardinge on Trench to Lascelles, Confidential, encl. in Lascelles to Grey, No. 58, 6 Feb. 1907, F.O. 367/42.

[45] Trench to Lascelles, 6 Feb. 1907. The head of the African Department, E. A. W. Clarke, noted: 'I have no doubt that the constant irritation which the Germans must feel at seeing the only good harbour of their huge colony in our possession has a good deal to do with their unfriendly attitude to-wards us in South Africa'. Minute by Clarke, 11 Feb. 1907, F.O. 367/42.

[46] Minute by Grey, c. 11 Feb. 1907, F.O. 367/42.

But what would Germany yield in exchange? Sir Eyre Crowe pointed out time and again in this and other instances that the Germans had little of value to offer in return. Moreover, 'the history of former transactions should make us chary of entering upon any bargaining with her [Germany]'. The permanent officials of the last decade of Anglo-German colonial relations before the war were determined to stop the trend of what they considered Germany's taking and Britain's giving. As Bertie, the Ambassador in Paris, wrote of 'German land hunger' in Africa in 1912: 'I am against giving up anything unless in return, not for words or even so-called deeds, but for solid territorial advantages for England'.[47]

Even with Walfisch Bay remaining firmly in British hands, 'German South-West' nevertheless seemed to jeopardize South Africa, and remained one of the main British concerns in the years before the outbreak of the war. The colony had become a haven for Boer rebels. Hardinge feared that the German railway might be used 'as a jumping off ground for raids into the most disaffected portion of Cape Colony'.[48] Nor were the Boers and the railway the only South-West African anxieties of the Foreign Office. Despite the German colonial reforms of the Dernburg era, the British officials feared the consequences of German native policy. In part this concern arose out of self-interest, because the Herero uprising of 1904 had created border difficulties; in part it arose out of humanitarian instinct. According to a British report in 1909:

The great aim of German policy in German South-West Africa, as regards the native, is to reduce him to a state of serfdom, and, where he resists, to destroy him altogether. The native, to the German, is a baboon and nothing more. The war against the Hereros, conduct-ed by General Trotha, was one of extermination; hundreds—men, women and children—were driven into desert country, where death from thirst was their end; whose [sic] left over are now in great locations near Windhuk, where they eke out a miserable existence; labour is forced upon them and naturally is unwillingly performed.[49]

[47] Bertie to Tyrrell, Private (copy), 26 Jan. 1912, F.O. 800/179, Bertie Papers.
[48] Minute by Hardinge on Trench to Lascelles, 26 Feb. 1907, encl. in Lascelles to Grey, No. 80, 1 Mar. 1907, F.O. 367/41.
[49] Captain H. S. P. Simon, 'Report on German South-West Africa', 6 Apr. 1909, F.O. 367/136.

On that report Sir Edward Grey noted: 'As bad as the Congo'.

The same combination of self-interest and humanitarianism dominated British Congo policy. At one stage Grey thought King Leopold's 'rubber atrocities' so bad that he considered the possibility of allowing France and Germany to partition the Congo between them. But to the Germanophobes of the Foreign Office this path seemed suicidal. Bertie wrote from Paris in November 1907:

I believe that the ambition and ultimate aim of Germany is to extend her African Possessions from sea to sea, viz., from the Indian Ocean to the South Atlantic. . . . if we begin by disclaiming all territorial desires we leave the cake to be cut up between France and Germany, and if later on we make objection to a prospective allotment between those two powers France would have reason to say you told me that so long as the natives were secured in their rights and the Berlin Act trade arrangements were observed you had no desires. What have you to complain of?[50]

Confronted with such views as those, Grey modified his stand. If the Congo State were 'cut up', the Foreign Office would evaluate British strategic and commercial interests in the Congo and act accordingly. In the words of the head of the African Department, Britain would object to 'anything which would enable Germany to bar the way definitely between our possessions in the South and Egypt and the Sudan'.[51]

Belgium's annexation of the Congo in 1908 did not end speculation about the future of central Africa. The British Congo reformers, if not the Foreign Office, regarded the Belgians as inferior colonialists who had neither the resources nor the abilities to administer the Congo. The Secretary of the Congo Reform Association, E. D. Morel, believed that the best solution to the problem of the Congo would be for Germany to take over most of it.

. . . Germany's line of natural overseas development is the Belgian Congo and Angola, a great central African State joining up with German East Africa across the Continent; with a neutral strip in the middle as from north to south and east to west. . . . Germany,

[50] Memorandum by Bertie, 25 Nov. 1907, Private, F.O. 367/74.
[51] Minute by Clarke, 2 Dec. 1907, on Bertie's memorandum of 25 Nov. 1907, F.O. 367/74. On Anglo-German rivalry in the Congo see especially Jacques Willequet, *Le Congo Belge et la Weltpolitik* (Brussels, 1962).

with British co-operation should work quietly at purchasing the bulk of the Belgian Congo and Angola. . . . It is a dream; but then, some dreams come true.[52]

A pro-German radical, Morel nevertheless commanded a powerful and articulate pressure group. His ideas coincided more or less with those of the German colonial enthusiasts who advocated the creation of a central African German empire stretching from the Atlantic to the Indian Ocean. During the Moroccan crisis of 1911 Germany took the first step towards this *Mittelafrika* by demanding the French Congo. As in the crisis of 1905–06, Germany backed down, receiving in the end only two thin strips of French equatorial territory bordering the Cameroons. Tropical Africa had once more proved its value as a safety valve in international relations; an explosion had been averted by letting the Germans blow off steam and acquire two worthless strips of jungle. It was a cheap price to pay to avoid war. But the arrangement did give Germany access to the Congo river. And the new territories pointed like 'antennae' towards the Belgian Congo.

In the case of the Belgian colonial possession, the Foreign Office after the annexation of 1908 became increasingly reluctant to intervene. Though Britain did not recognize the Belgian annexation until 1913, the Belgian reforms destroyed any excuse for interference. The Foreign Office moreover feared that an aggressive Congo policy might drive Belgium into the arms of Germany. The Portuguese colonies were a different matter. '. . . The Germans would like the division of the Portuguese Colonies to take place as soon as possible', Grey wrote in December 1911:

So should I. These Colonies are worse than derelict so long as Portugal has them: [they are sinks of iniquity]: the Union of South Africa will never rest till it has Delagoa Bay: on every ground material and moral and even Portuguese it would be better that Portugal should sell her Colonies.[53]

[52] Morel to Holt, 7 Oct. 1912, Morel Papers, London School of Economics.

[53] Grey to Goschen, Private (copy), 29 Dec. 1911, F.O. 800/61, Grey Papers. The bracketed phrase was omitted in the copy published in *British Documents*, X, 2, p. 424, 'for reasons of international courtesy'.

Grey opened negotiations with the Germans in order to bring the 1898 agreement up to date. By doing so he hoped to prove, in the tradition of Granville and Salisbury, that Britain did not begrudge Germany's colonial ambitions. By redrawing the 1898 arrangement more in Germany's favour, he believed that he might again demonstrate Britain's willingness to accommodate Germany in colonial regions. An agreement was initialled in August 1913. But it was never signed. As a condition to the treaty Grey insisted that it be published along with the ones of 1898 and 1899. He could thus demonstrate that he had not been guilty of 'secret diplomacy'; that he bore no responsibility for the origins of the transaction (by throwing the blame on Salisbury); and that he would not be privy to seizing the colonies without Portuguese consent. The Germans began to suspect that Grey was guilty of duplicity in the same way, from their point of view, that Salisbury had been in 1899. In the end, Grey, perhaps unwittingly, took the same stand as Salisbury. 'The position I seemed to assume', the German Ambassador told him, 'was that of the medical adviser to the Portuguese Colonies, while what Germany contemplated was that of being the heir'.[54] Final agreement was never reached. The outbreak of the First World War interrupted the last experiment in Anglo-German colonial 'cooperation'.

The British Government justified the negotiations with the Germans on grounds of 'Portuguese slavery'. The Foreign Office no less than the humanitarians believed that Portuguese rule was both corrupt and cruel, and that the Portuguese colonies would be much better off under British sway. But— why did the Foreign Office as well as the humanitarian societies choose to attack Portuguese and Belgian 'atrocities' and ignore abuses in German colonies? It is a curious commentary on British humanitarianism that one of the main supporters of the Congo reform movement, the Liverpool West African trader, John Holt, asked in 1909: 'Is it true that the Germans butchered the Hererros [sic]—men, women and children. . . ? I have never heard of this before'.[55] The Foreign Office was well aware of this humanitarian blindspot. One official commented in August 1912:

[54] *British Documents*, X, 2, p. 535.
[55] Holt to Morel, 5 Oct. 1909, Morel Papers.

In view of the cruelty, treachery & commercialism by which the German colonial authorities have gradually reduced their natives to the status of cattle (without so much of a flutter being caused among English peace-loving philanthropists) the [Portuguese] S. Thomé agitation in its later phases against a weak & silly nation without resources is the more sickening. These Hereros were butchered by thousands during the war & have been ruthlessly flogged into subservience since.[56]

In justice to the humanitarians, some did protest against the treatment of the Hereros. But it is a historical fact that before the war the British concentrated most of their humanitarian energy on exposing the maladministration in Belgian and Portuguese Africa and paid little attention to abuses in German territories. Far from denouncing the Germans as inferior colonial rulers, most Englishmen held them in some esteem. They admired the efficient way in which the Germans administered their colonies, the railway building, the research stations, the public works, the roads—in short, the energy and resourcefulness with which the Germans were developing their overseas territories. According to the popular notion, the British and German races seemed to be in ascendancy, the French, Belgian and Portuguese races in decline. The colonies of Belgium and Portugal, if not those of France, would eventually fall to the great and superior Empires of Britain and Germany. The reason seemed clear: the Belgians and the Portuguese had forfeited their 'moral right' to colonies because of cruelty to the indigenous inhabitants—the same argument which was used during the war against the Germans. During the course of the war the British public heard much about German 'colonial atrocities'. But if an opinion poll had been taken in England before August 1914, the result probably would have been that the Germans were regarded as better colonial rulers than any others except the British.

[56] Minute by F. E. F. Adam, 20 Aug. 1912, F.O. 367/276. The Foreign Office itself did not protest against either German or French maladministration; in the words of the head of the African Department (in a different context): 'In the first place ... au fond the French and Germans are reasonably civilized creatures and in the next ... France and Germany are boys too big to interfere with. It may be quite possible and one's duty to prevent a big boy bullying a small but it is quite another matter to stop a strong man beating a little'. Minute by Clarke, 21 Dec. 1906, F.O. 367/5.

G.L.C.—4

II. CONQUEST
1914–1916

THE fate of the German colonies was foreshadowed on 5 August 1914, the day after Britain's declaration of war against Germany. Assembling in London under the auspices of the Committee of Imperial Defence, a group of British military and colonial experts—aptly known as the 'Offensive Sub-Committee'—decided to carry the European struggle to Africa and the Pacific by launching military operations against the German colonies. H. H. Asquith, the Prime Minister, assented, thus initiating a series of colonial campaigns in which British troops eventually conquered most of Germany's overseas territories.[1]

British command of the seas made the German colonies a natural target; but protection of British sea-power was the primary aim. 'All operations', according to the official naval history, 'were to be regarded primarily as designed for the defence of our maritime communications and not for territorial conquest'.[2] The German cables and coaling stations in the Pacific, the cruisers that roved the Indian ocean and frequented the coast of East Africa, the long range wireless telegraph station in South-West Africa, the radio-telegraphy post in Togoland—the entire system of German colonial communications and naval forces that depended on them: these the authorities in London regarded as a menace both to Britain's control of the seas and protection of her colonial territories. The public in the Dominions as well as in England acutely

[1] 'Proceedings of a Sub-Committee of the Committee of Imperial Defence, assembled on the 5th. of August, 1914, to consider the question of offensive operations against German Colonies', Secret, Asquith Papers. Asquith's marginal 'yeses' on this memorandum form his only substantial contribution to the decisions made about the future of the German colonies. The Cabinet approved of the committee's recommendations the next day. On the work of the Offensive Sub-Committee, see especially Sir Julian Corbett and Sir Henry Newbolt, *Naval Operations* (5 vols., London, 1920–31), I, p. 128 ff. Also Lord Hankey, *The Supreme Command, 1914–1918* (2 vols., London, 1961), I, pp. 168–9; and Paul Guinn, *British Strategy and Politics, 1914 to 1918* (Oxford, 1965), p. 41. Guinn's book, which has an extensive bibliography, is the best recent work on British strategy during the war.

[2] *Naval Operations*, I, p. 129.

perceived this danger. According to an Australian newspaper, the Melbourne *Age:*

Every German colony has a powerful wireless station—they will talk to one another across the seas, and at every opportunity they [German ships] will dash from cover to harry and destroy our commerce, and maybe, to raid our coasts.[3]

In the newspapers at this time ran the theme that Germany had planted strategic colonies in the Pacific and Africa to use them eventually as bases for attack against British territories. Especially to Australians, New Zealanders and South Africans, one of the main goals of the war was to destroy Germany's 'place in the sun', thereby securing their own safety. 'Security' remained the British colonial watchword throughout the war.

*   *   *

In the Pacific, Australasian and Japanese forces captured the German colonies within four months after the outbreak of war. The main events were these. On 15 August Japan presented an ultimatum to Germany consisting of two demands: the withdrawal of German men-of-war from Chinese and Japanese waters; and the cession of the leased territory of Kiaochow 'with a view to the eventual restoration of the same to China'. The Germans did not respond. Japan on 23 August declared war and began the siege of Kiaochow, an operation not completed until early November after 1,800 Japanese casualties and the death of 200 Germans. On 30 August approximately 1,000 New Zealand troops occupied Samoa. The Germans there capitulated without resistance. The Australians, about 1,600 men in force, hoisted the British flag on German New Guinea on 13 September after some sharp fighting with German troops.[4] On 7 October the Japanese, despite declarations that their manoeuvers would be confined to Chinese and Japanese waters, for 'strategic' reasons occupied the Marshalls and Carolines; during the rest of the month they took the remaining German

---

[3] 12 Aug. 1914.

[4] News of the Australasian movements in the Pacific was subjected to heavy censorship, especially in Australia. The Australian press, for example, learned of the capture of Samoa from an American newspaper. There has not been much written about this problem, but see an unpublished University of Melbourne thesis by D. C. S. Sissons, 'Attitudes to Japan and Defence, 1890–1923' (1956), *passim.*

islands north of the Equator.[5] The subsequent destruction in various battles of the German cruisers *Emden, Scharnhorst, Gneisenau, Leipzig* and *Dresden* ended German naval power in the Pacific.[6] 'With the British fleet in command of the seas', commented the Perth *Daily News,* 'Germany's hopes of colonial expansion must remain barren'. But only with Japanese support did the British manage to retain control of the seas. The military operations in the Pacific demonstrated the extent to which the security of the British Empire itself as well as that of the Australasian Dominions depended on Japanese sea power. In their war against Germany, the British now reaped the benefits of the alliance concluded over a decade earlier with Japan. Even Australians, with their traditional hostility towards the Japanese, began to see the value of the Anglo-Japanese alliance. According to the *West Australian:*

It is no secret that the Alliance has not in the past been viewed with whole-souled enthusiasm by every section of the Australian people; to-day it is highly important, for the sake of our national future, that we should venture upon some clear and cool thinking on this matter, and that we should look at the facts, not through a veil of sentiment and prejudice, but face to face. . . . Britain has paralysed German oversea commerce, and has kept her own trade routes clear, because she was able, in good time, to call her ships home to guard her own gateways; and it was the Japanese Alliance which enabled her to do this.[7]

According to the Adelaide *Register,* Japan had 'extinguished all hopes of German aggression in the Pacific, and materially

[5] The two most important unpublished British documents which trace the evolution of Japanese aims in the Pacific are by C. Wing, 'Memorandum on the Japanese Occupation of Pacific Islands', Confidential, 22 Dec. 1915, F.O. 371/2689, and one circulated by Lord Robert Cecil to the War Cabinet, Confidential, 15 Oct. 1918, F.O. 371/3236.

[6] These events may be followed by reading the official Australian history of the war in the Pacific by S. S. Mackenzie, *The Australians at Rabaul: the Capture and Administration of the German Possessions in the Southern Pacific* (Sydney, 1938). Russell H. Fifield illuminates the problem of Japanese expansion in the Pacific as well as in China from the point of view of American foreign policy in *Woodrow Wilson and the Far East: the Diplomacy of the Shantung Question* (New York, 1952); see also another valuable work along the same lines, Roy Watson Curry, *Woodrow Wilson and Far Eastern Policy, 1913–1921* (New York, 1957). For naval engagements see especially Arthur J. Marder, *From the Dreadnought to Scapa Flow* (2 vols., London, 1961–65), II, chap. VI.

[7] 10 Oct. 1914.

added to the safety of British colonies and trade in Eastern waters'.[8] In London *The Times* referred to the Japanese as 'a chivalrous and an honourable people upholding the principles of civilization in the Far East'.[9]

The British nevertheless watched the expansion of the Japanese into the Pacific with misgiving. The islands occupied by them consisted of the Carolines, Ladrones (Marianas), Marshall and Pelew (Palau) groups—all north of 'the Line', but near enough to arouse Australasian anxiety. 'We would feel safer', commented the New Zealand Invercargill *Southland Times*, 'with the Pacific islands under the flag of a white Power than under the emblem of the Rising Sun.'[10] Nor were the New Zealanders and Australians the only ones alarmed at Japanese movements in the Pacific. 'The Americans', as one Foreign Office official noted, 'are as suspicious as our own Colonies.'[11] The Australasians feared the 'Japanese Peril' in the north; the Americans apprehended the danger—which materialized during the Second World War—of allowing the Japanese to come closer to the Philippines and Hawaii. With one eye cocked towards the Dominions and the United States, and the other towards Japan, the Foreign Secretary, Sir Edward Grey, saw that the question of an eventual settlement in the Pacific would pose immense problems.[12]

Grey recognized that the Japanese eventually would get a share of the spoils. 'It cannot be expected', he wrote two weeks after Britain's entry into the war, 'that Japan will spend blood & treasure in Kiao-Chou & get nothing for it—not even the remains of the German lease'.[13] But he resisted Japanese efforts to obtain an explicit understanding that they should retain the territories taken by them. In deference to him the Japanese were willing to make public pronouncements that their occupation 'will be without prejudice to final arrangements'; they nevertheless informed the British Ambassador in

[8] 23 Sept. 1914.   [9] 14 Dec. 1914.   [10] 18 Aug. 1914.
[11] Minute by W. Langley, *c.* 8 Oct. 1914 (57114), F.O. 371/2017. See also minute by B. Alston commenting on the excitement caused in America by the Japanese occupation of the islands: 'This is very ridiculous of the Americans. These islands have been the chief naval base, coaling station &c of the Scharnhorst, Gneisenau & Emden, and their seizure was an imperative military necessity'. 7 Oct. 1914 (56653), *ibid.*
[12] See especially Grey's minutes in the F.O. 371 Japan series.
[13] Minute by Grey, *c.* 19 Aug. 1914 (40679), F.O. 371/2019.

Tokyo that they would 'naturally insist on retaining permanently all the German islands lying north of [the] equator'
and would rely on British support.[14] Commenting on the in-
consistency of that position, one of the Japanese experts of the
Foreign Office, B. Alston, pointed out that Britain could not
formally acknowledge Japan's claims without taking the Allies
and the United States into account.

It is clear that the Japanese must have compensation somewhere in
the Pacific—and there seems no very grave objection from *our* point
of view—though there may be grave objection from the American
point of view—to their keeping some, if not all, these Islands north
of the Equator—but in view of our engagement with France &
Russia we must decline to be drawn into any engagement of support
to any definite Japanese claim when terms of peace are discussed.[15]

Grey had this answer to the problem:

... Japan must have compensation after the war proportionate to
her efforts, but . . . with regard to all territory conquered & newly
occupied during the war the only acceptable basis is that it should
be without prejudice to final arrangements to be made in time of
peace & we propose to apply this to all territory *not* previously
occupied by ourselves before the war.[16]

The Japanese at this stage did not press the issue; but they left
no doubt that at the peace settlement they would expect
Grey's 'good offices'. From Grey's point of view that attitude
was satisfactory because he could avoid, temporarily at least,
a secret pledge to Japan that might offend the United States
and the Australasian Dominions.[17] Until the concluding of the
Anglo-Japanese agreement of 1917 the Foreign Office managed
not to commit themselves.

[14] Greene to Grey, No. 241 tel., 1 Dec. 1914, F.O. 371/2018.
[15] Minute by Alston, 17 Dec. 1914 (83612), F.O. 371/2018.
[16] Minute by Grey, c. 17 Dec. 1914 (83612), F.O. 371/2018.
[17] Harcourt repeatedly gave the Australians official and private assurances that the Imperial Government had not concluded a secret agreement
with Japan. For example, he telegraphed to Ferguson in February 1915:
'we have no arrangement or understanding secret or otherwise with the
Japanese Government about Islands in the Pacific except that the occupation of all territory conquered during the war by the Allies is to be without
prejudice [to] final arrangement to be made in terms [of] peace at the end
of the war'. Harcourt to Ferguson, Secret, 23 Feb. 1915, Governor-General's
Office, 89/68: C.P. 78/23, Commonwealth Archives Office.

Had the Australians not been so 'dilatory'[18] in their assault against the German islands the Japanese might not have had the chance to occupy them. Considering the vast distances of the Pacific, the presence of German cruisers, the size of the Australian navy and the unexpected outbreak of the war, that implication is probably unfair;[19] in any case the fault did not lie with the Imperial Government. Two days after Britain's declaration of war the Colonial Secretary, Lewis Harcourt, had telegraphed to the southern Dominions that it would be a 'great and urgent Imperial service' if they would seize the German colonies in their vicinity.[20] Yet almost an entire month elapsed before New Zealand troops, escorted by the Australian navy, arrived at Samoa.[21] Another two weeks passed before the Australians attacked Rabaul and New Guinea. Finally in late November they considered extending their operations north of the Line. On the 25th of that month, the Governor-General, Sir Ronald Munro Ferguson, telegraphed the Colonial Office in London inquiring whether the Australian expeditionary force in the Pacific should proceed northwards. Harcourt replied on 3 December that he would be 'glad' if the Australians would confine their operations to the islands south of the Equator.[22] Three days later he gave this explanation to Ferguson:

[18] The word used by Alston in a minute of 30 Oct. 1914 (64641), F.O. 371/2018.

[19] But see Ferguson's remarks to Harcourt: 'the difficulty of understanding naval strategy in the Pacific is giving rise to criticisms. It is thought that a capital mistake was made in sending an expedition to Samoa before the wireless N.E. of Australia was dealt with, and the enemy chased from the Sea; also that for some days past H.M.A. Ships in the Bismarck Archipelago have been wasted'. (Ferguson to Harcourt, Personal [copy], 29 Sept. 1914, Novar Papers).

[20] '. . . Harcourt as Colonial Secretary had of his own initiative, and as far as I know without consulting anyone, communicated with the various Dominions and Colonies with a view to their taking action'. Hankey, *Supreme Command*, I, pp. 168–9.

[21] The Governor-General of Australia reported to the Colonial Secretary: 'the occupation of Samoa by New Zealand rankles a little. It is felt that she got there thanks to the protection of the Australian Fleet, and can only remain there under the same protection. Australia regards the Pacific as her "duck-pond" and scarcely admits New Zealand's right to a look-in'. (Ferguson to Harcourt, Personal [copy], 13 May 1915, Novar Papers). Throughout the war the Australians showed a far more intense interest in the Pacific islands than did the New Zealanders.

[22] 'Pelew, Marianne, Caroline Islands and Marshall Islands are at present in military occupation by Japanese who are at our request engaged

aphed to you on the 3rd[23] that in view of the fact that the
...se are in actual occupation of the German Pacific Islands
north of the Equator, and in view of the great assistance they are
rendering to us (at our request) with their fleet through the *whole*
of the Pacific, it seemed to us here undesirable that the Australian
Expedition should proceed anywhere north of the Equator at the
present time. . . .

I feel that I ought to give you *personally* some explanation . . . but
I must impress upon you that this letter is for your eye only, and
under no circumstances is to be seen by anyone else. . . .

Our fleets were so fully engaged in the North Sea, Atlantic,
Mediterranean, and in convoy of troops across the Indian Ocean
that we could not spare enough to deal with the Pacific. We had
therefore to call in Japanese aid. . . .

It has even been in contemplation (and still is) that the Japanese
fleet may in the future be employed in the European theatre of war.

All this has changed the character of the Japanese participation
and no doubt of their eventual claims to compensation.

There is a considerable agitation in Japan against the present
Govt. on the ground that they are giving much and getting nothing.
. . .

From information which reaches me I have very little doubt that
it is the intention of the Japanese at the end of the war to claim
for themselves all the German Islands North of the Equator. Of
course we should absolutely refuse at this present time to make any
admission of such a claim.

Our attitude throughout has been that all these territorial questions must be settled in the terms of peace and not before.

But it would be impossible at this moment to risk a quarrel with
our Ally which would be the certain & immediate result of any
attempt diplomatically to oust them now from those islands which
they are occupying more or less at the invitation of the Admiralty.
. . .

All this is a long story . . . but the moral of it is that you ought
in the most gradual & diplomatic way to begin to prepare the mind
of your Ministers for the possibility that at the end of the war Japan

in policing waters Northern Pacific. We consider it most convenient for
strategic reasons to allow them to remain in occupation for the present
leaving whole question of future to be settled at the end of war. We should
be glad therefore if the Australian expedition would confine itself to occupation of German Islands South of the Equator'. Harcourt to Ferguson,
Secret, cablegram, 3 Dec. 1914, Governor-General's Office, 89/68: C.P.
78/23, Commonwealth Archives Office.

[23] i.e. the cablegram quoted in the preceding footnote.

may be left in possession of the Northern Islands and we with everything south of the Equator.

I know that they won't like this, but after all the thing of most importance are those territories most contiguous to Australia, and it will be a great gain to add German New Guinea to Papua and to have the whole of the Solomon Isl. group under the British flag.

I fear I have set you a hard task but I am sure you will execute it with your usual skill & discretion. . . . [24]

Ferguson—whom Walter Long (Colonial Secretary December 1916–January 1919) judged to be one of the great Governor-Generals in the history of the British Empire—had anticipated Harcourt's request. 'I am glad to be able to say', he wrote in January 1915, 'that I had already done something in the direction of meeting your wishes re the post bellum Pacific situation, and in talking over the question with trustworthy leading men had suggested the Equator as a likely line between British and Japanese Spheres in the Pacific'. He went on:

When our Ally's Fleet went to the Carolines and Mariannes it seemed unlikely that it would again evacuate those Islands. . . . I therefore sounded those with whom I am on confidential terms in naval, military and political circles . . . as to their views on the matter. None of these showed much antipathy to the suggestion—though we agreed our fractious U.S.A. Coz. wouldn't like it. They all rather accepted it as an inevitable sequence to the inestimable service rendered by Japan to Australia throughout the War. [25]

Though accepting the Japanese occupation of the islands north of the Equator as an accomplished fact, the Australians continued to be 'jumpy', as Ferguson put it, about the 'Yellow Peril Scare'.[26] Japan's '21 Demands' of January-June 1915 again conjured up the spectre of Japanese expansion; and with it the fear that the Carolines eventually might be used as a 'jumping off place' against Australia. The New Zealanders shared the same concern, as is illustrated by the following excerpts from a secret despatch written by the Governor

[24] Harcourt to Ferguson, Private & Personal, Very Secret, 6 Dec. 1914, Novar Papers; copy in the Harcourt Papers.
[25] Ferguson to Harcourt, Personal, 20 Jan. 1915, Harcourt Papers; copy in the Novar Papers.
[26] Ferguson to Harcourt, Personal, 31 May 1915, Harcourt papers; copy in the Novar Papers.

in Wellington, Lord Liverpool. Summarizing the views of his Ministers, he wrote:

That the New Zealand Government . . . should always ask His Majesty's Government to use every effort to prevent the advance of the frontier of Japan in the Pacific. . . .

That if it is found necessary to leave Japan in possession, it should be definitely agreed that none of the islands should be fortified or used as a coaling station or naval base. . . .

That neither Australia nor New Zealand will ever be convinced that in the future our peril is not from Japan, and the New Zealand Government would only ask the Imperial Government not to adopt the contrary view. . . .

If the Imperial Government, however, tells the New Zealand Government that their views are wrong as to the future danger . . . [then] the Imperial Government . . . can never expect assent, but, on the contrary, must be prepared for bitter resentment.[27]

Discussing similar sentiments of his Australian Ministers, Ferguson said that the real danger was not the islands in the Pacific but the 'White Australia' policy and its corollary of encouraging people mainly of English stock to colonize Australia. 'It leaves us an empty continent, while it invites occupation by other peoples. This fool's paradise needs a rude awakening, and if a Japanese naval base near the Line should act as a solvent then it would be a blessing in disguise!'[28]

[27] Liverpool to Harcourt, Most Secret, 13 May 1915, C.O. 537/1173. Note the Foreign Office comment on this despatch: 'It is evident that the future negotiations of the Far Eastern section of the Peace settlement will have a very thorny path to tread. . . . It is no good attempting to convince either Australians or New Zealanders either in their public or private capacities that the "Japanese peril" from a *political* point of view is largely a figment of their imaginations. The Japanese are not naturally a colonizing race. . . . Australian fears are exaggerated on that score, while China will offer for many years to come a far more tempting field for political adventure and one in which the ground is already prepared. All the Japanese really want in Australia & New Zealand is a field to which the cheap Japanese labourer can go for a few years and then return to Japan to settle down on his savings. To allow this would naturally be unpleasing to the Australian working man & to the Government he elects, but it does not follow that it would necessarily be a . . . disaster from the Imperial point of view—the Japanese are excellent workmen!' (84478), 26 Aug. 1915, F.O. 371/2382.

[28] Ferguson to Harcourt, Personal, 6 Apr. 1915, Harcourt Papers; copy in Novar Papers. Did Japanese occupation of the Carolines jeopardize Australian security? See my article in the *Journal of Modern History*, XXXVIII (Dec. 1966).

Ferguson's opinion was not shared by the Australians themselves. In particular W. M. Hughes, who became Prime Minister of Australia in October 1915, feared that British diplomacy might encourage the Japanese to think that the 'White Australia' policy and commercial restrictions might be relaxed. During his trip to England in 1916 he reported with alarm the gist of his conversations with Grey.

> The position is aggravated—I will not say it is critical—by the fact that Britain has approached Japan with a view to obtaining naval (and, or, military assistance)—say in the Mediterranean—and that the Japanese Government, while ready to grant this, asks for some evidence of Britain's friendliness to her in order possibly to justify her action or placate the opposition. And, as Grey says,—if we say: Well we are very friendly towards you and we want your aid to win this war—*but*—(1) you must not get any concessions in China: (2) your people cannot come to Australia: (3) you are not to be allowed most favoured nation treatment with Australia (or other parts of the Empire), Japan can hardly be expected to treat our protestations of friendship very seriously.[29]

Hughes had hit upon the heart of Britain's diplomatic difficulty in the Far East. To win the war Britain needed Japanese support. But the Japanese expected something in return. The British had little to give. Apart from the islands north of the equator, their hands were tied by Australasian sentiment. 'I told Grey', Hughes wrote, 'that Australia would fight to the last ditch rather than allow Japanese to enter Australia. Upon that point we were adamant'.[30]

Nor would the Australasians be prepared to hand back the German islands in case the war ended inconclusively. If Germany asked, as the price of her evacuation of Belgium, for the restoration of her colonies, the British Government would have to reply, according to a Foreign Office memorandum, that the ones in the Pacific had passed 'beyond recall' to Japan, Australia and New Zealand. The Germans might then retort that the British could give up some of their other colonial territories.[31]

[29] Hughes to Pearce, Strictly Confidential, 21 Apr. 1916, Pearce Papers, Australian National War Memorial, Canberra.
[30] *Ibid.*
[31] Memorandum by Ralph Paget and W. Tyrrell, 'Suggested Basis for a Territorial Settlement in Europe', Very Secret, G.-78, 7 Aug. 1916, Asquith Papers; CAB. 24/2.

In the words of the Chief of the Imperial War Staff, Sir William Robertson, 'we may be placed in a difficult position'. He continued:

> Kiauchau, the Marianne, Caroline and Marshall Islands have been occupied by and are being administered by, the Japanese, and Japan is unlikely to release her hold on them without a substantial *quid pro quo*, which it will not be easy to find.
>
> The Samoan Islands were occupied by, and are now administered by, the Government of New Zealand, which is likely to attach a high sentimental value to this, the first conquest of a young people. The same applies to German New Guinea, the Bismarck Archipelago and the Solomon Islands, which were occupied by and are now in the hands of the Australian Government, who have the further inducement, to keep what they have got, that these islands form a valuable buffer between the mainland and possible Japanese encroachment.[32]

Australia and New Zealand, not to mention Japan, would not surrender the German islands under their occupation except in case of total German victory, if then. The problem facing the Imperial Government throughout the war thus consisted of how to deal with Germany and Japan in the event of a peace imposed by the enemy, or one that remained inconclusive; or how to cope with Japan if the Allies won. The Australians were willing to acquiesce in Japan's permanent occupation of the islands north of the Equator.[33] But the Imperial as well as the Australasian Governments saw the danger of increasing Japanese power in the East. Japan, according to Ferguson, intended 'to follow in the footsteps of Germany . . . [on] this side of the World—where she evidently means to become the dominant power'.[34]

During Harcourt's tenure of office as Colonial Secretary— until May 1915—the Colonial Office took a firm lead as protector of British Australasian interests and began to consider ways of strengthening British influence in the Pacific. Harcourt

[32] Memorandum by Robertson, Secret, 30 Aug. 1916, Austen Chamberlain Papers.

[33] As early as 19 May 1915 Ferguson cabled Harcourt that the Australian Government would have no objection 'to continued occupation by Japanese of islands North of Line when question raised at end of war. . . '. (Ferguson to Harcourt, Secret and Personal [copy], cablegram, Novar Papers).

[34] Ferguson to Law, Personal (copy), 3 Aug. 1916, Novar Papers.

saw the Equator as a sharp line dividing the two spheres; but, in contrast to the highly centralized administration being established by the Japanese in the north, there was a loose conglomeration of British territories in the south. Harcourt wanted to tighten up this administration by placing certain islands such as the Solomons under Australian rather than Imperial control. He also proposed to improve relations with the French either by 'bribing' them to end the unhappy condominium in the New Hebrides in favour of the British or by giving them complete control in return for concessions elsewhere. When Bonar Law succeeded Harcourt, the initiative in propounding such schemes as those shifted to Ferguson, who attempted to plot long range British strategy in the Pacific. To offset increasing Japanese influence he thought Britain should bring another first-class power into the mainstream of Pacific affairs. One way of doing that, as Harcourt had suggested, would be to yield the British share of the New Hebrides to the French. 'It looks as if the Condominium had better be ended in their favour', Ferguson wrote to the Governor of Fiji (who also advocated this idea), 'in order to firmly establish a third Power in the Pacific and so end our tête-à-tête with Japan'.[35] Another way would be to strengthen the position of the United States in the Pacific, perhaps by letting the Americans take over the part of Samoa under the occupation of New Zealand.[36] As with similar ideas about a general shuffle of territories in Africa after the war, all those Pacific schemes failed, not least for local reasons. The British settlers in the New Hebrides no more wanted their administration transferred to the French than the New Zealanders desired to see Samoa ceded to the Americans— just as the Japanese had no intention of handing over the former German possessions under their control to the Australians.

[35] Ferguson to Sir Bicham Escott, Personal & Private (copy), 13 Jan. 1917, Novar Papers.
[36] This idea can be associated especially with the Governor of Fiji during a later stage of the war: 'for the same reason that it may be as well to strengthen the French in the New Hebrides', he wrote in 1918, 'I would strengthen also the U.S.A. by handing over to them entirely Samoa. We do not require Samoa for any special purpose, and we cannot expect to have everything when the war is over. Fiji would be a far better outlet than Samoa for the energies of New Zealand, if they find the limits of their own Dominion too confined. . . '. (Escott to Hughes, 4 May 1918, Hughes Papers).

In broad perspective the future of the Pacific and the Far East depended upon the intentions of the Japanese and the outcome of the war. In 1916 the Foreign Office feared that Japan might abandon Britain in favour of Germany—an event that could have resulted in military defeat of the Allies and territorial losses for the British throughout the world. In return for acknowledging German hegemony in Europe, the Middle East and Africa, the Japanese might have received a free hand in the Pacific, China, South-East Asia—including the Dutch East Indies—and even India.[37] Some rumours that reached the Foreign Office included the speculation that the Japanese might be entertaining a proposed alliance with the Germans in order to clear the way for an attack on the Australasian Dominions and 'to annex California'. Grey in conversations with the Japanese Ambassador in London tried to laugh off those possibilities as somewhat 'amusing'.[38] In fact the Foreign Office staff was alarmed. Even if a German–Japanese rapprochement did not occur during the war, it might afterwards. 'We cannot exclude the possibility', Alston minuted, 'of an Alliance between Japan & Germany after the war, for a reconstruction of the situation in the Far East'. He went on:

It is quite plain that since the taking of Kiaochow nothing has been neglected to assuage German feelings & to prove that Japan having acted in accordance with her Treaty requirements is animated by the greatest admiration for German ability & resource. The quarrel between Japan & Germany is not a deep one, & owing to present conditions in Europe, Germany is Japan's least dangerous competitor in the Far East today. Calculating that the present war will not leave Germany on the best of terms with any of the Allies with whom Japan herself is immediately concerned, the Govt. of Tokio may see an opportunity for an Alliance there which does not present itself elsewhere.[39]

[37] The India Office and Foreign Office at this stage of the war were greatly disturbed about a possible increase of Japanese commercial and eventual political influence in India. See especially the despatches and minutes Grey ordered to be kept 'very secret' in F.O. 371/2693.

[38] Grey to Greene, No. 29 Very Secret (draft), 24 Jan. 1916, F.O. 371/2690.

[39] Minute by Alston, 30 Mar. 1916 (52498), F.O. 371/2691. See also various minutes in the same series written by Lord Robert Cecil and other members of the Foreign Office staff who compared the military and political methods of Japan with those of Germany. See for example Cecil's minute written in early May 1916 (83294), F.O. 371/2693.

During the course of 1916 British apprehension about a possible German–Japanese alliance subsided when the Japanese judged that the war was turning in favour of the Allies—the decisive event in Japanese eyes apparently being the battle of Jutland in June. The uneasy Anglo–Japanese partnership continued, perhaps mainly because of the sort of assurances given by Grey to the Japanese Ambassador: 'if Japan did not pursue expansion in Europe, America, or Africa, the Powers who did expand in these Continents ought to be favourable to the expansion of Japanese influence and interest in the Far East'.[40] As Lord Hardinge, the Permanent Under-Secretary of the Foreign Office, summed up the situation: 'it is essential to humour Japan during the progress of the war, but at its close it will be necessary to arrive at a distinct understanding as to our own and Japanese interests in the Far East'.[41] Compared with the large question of the future balance of power in the Far East, the small one of the future of the German colonies in the Pacific seemed insignificant.

Long before the close of 1916 even the Governments of the antipodean Dominions had reconciled themselves to the idea of permanent Japanese occupation of the islands north of the Equator. The public in England and in Australasia knew nothing, of course, of the secret discussions between the British and Japanese Governments that eventually led to the Anglo–Japanese agreement of February 1917. But the press regarded Japan's annexation of the islands as the inevitable price to be paid for her contribution to the Allies' cause—just as newspaper opinion in England as well as in the Dominions considered it equitable that Australia, New Zealand and South Africa should retain the colonial territories conquered by them in the Pacific and in South-West Africa. These campaigns had been fought to make the Empire secure against German aggression. In the process British colonial troops had carried the standard of liberty and civilization to the former colonies of the 'Hun'. Those were the two themes of public opinion in Australasia as well as in South Africa and England. At the beginning of the

---

[40] Grey to Greene, No. 29 Very Secret (draft), 24 Jan. 1916, F.O. 371/2690.

[41] Minute by Hardinge, c. 3 Jan. 1917 (263898), F.O. 371/2693. In this regard, see Frank W. Iklé, 'Japanese-German Peace Negotiations during World War I', *American Historical Review*, LXXI (Oct. 1965).

war the Adelaide *Advertiser* had commented: 'there is no Power
which has failed more lamentably in colonisation than Germany,
with her drill-sergeant methods of enforcing her authority . . .
successful government requires not the mailed fist, but the light
hand'.[42] The Australians and New Zealanders no less than other
British subjects were convinced of the justice of their imperial
cause and the superiority of their colonial rule. 'In this present
war', commented the Melbourne *Age* in 1916, 'the British
Empire is fighting not only for the rights of small European
States, but also . . . for the rights of coloured people throughout
the world'.[43]

*   *   *

In Africa the outbreak of war touched off a series of border
skirmishes. Some of them developed into large scale colonial
campaigns, some did not. German troops in Togoland capitulated almost immediately; those in German East Africa did not
lay down their arms until after the armistice. South-West
Africa fell in July 1915, the Cameroons in February of the next
year. The British press regarded the West African campaigns
as trivial; the ones in South-West and East Africa caught the
public's eye. If Germany conspired against British authority
the world over, the latter two colonies were especially dangerous.
From East Africa, so it was believed, the Germans might launch
an attack against Britain's jewel, India; from South-West
Africa, against the lynchpin of the Empire, the Cape. Those
stereotyped thoughts may seem exaggerated in retrospect, but
many believed them to be realistic at the time.

South-West Africa in particular seemed to jeopardize British
colonial hegemony—a view not entirely removed from reality,
at least in southern Africa. The Union Prime Minister, Louis
Botha, supported by his Minister of Defence, J. C. Smuts,
immediately planned an invasion of the neighbouring German
colony. The border warfare which broke out between South-
West African and Union troops in September apparently
justified Botha's and Harcourt's view that the taking of the
German colony was a South African as well as an Imperial

[42] 1 Sept. 1914.   [43] 5 Feb. 1916.

'service'.[44] By engaging South African forces against German ones, however, Botha faced the charge that he might be fighting for British imperialism rather than for the interests of his fellow Afrikaners. He tried to offset that suspicion by enlisting only volunteers for the South-West African campaign; and the vote of confidence given him by the South African Parliament seemed to prove that the Afrikaners as well as the English in South Africa believed in the justice of the British cause. In fact the war threatened to disrupt the uneasy peace between the two communities.[45] On 9 October Colonel S. G. Maritz of the Union army precipitated an Afrikaner rebellion by defecting to the Germans.[46] The rebellion was the most important colonial event of the First World War. The British faced the prospect of re-fighting the Boer War at the same time that they struggled for their existence on the western front.

Harcourt was so alarmed that he tentatively planned to divert Australian troops on their way to the Dardanelles to South Africa to help suppress the rising. He sent the following 'Private & personal & most secret' telegram to Lord Buxton, the Governor-General, on 23 October:

Australian & New Zealand contingents of 30,000 men are leaving Adelaide, will coal at Mauritius and then proceed here via the Cape. They will not reach the Cape for about a month. If the situation required it at that time they might be called upon to assist the Union Govt. You should mention this to Botha and impress upon him need of extreme secrecy. No one knows of the diversion of the Australian convoy from Suez to Cape route. You should make it

[44] See Harcourt's telegram referred to in note 20 above; and Botha's speech reported in *The Times*, 11 Sept. 1914. 'Botha told me [Hankey] . . . that it had always been his intention, if war broke out, to be the first man to enter German South-West Africa at the head of an army, as its capture would be essential to the stability of the Union'. (Hankey, *Supreme Command*, I, p. 168). Botha's attitude was more complex than Hankey implies: 'General Botha was somewhat nervous about the political position, especially in regard to the German South West African expedition, which is not at all popular with a certain section of his Dutch supporters; who, while perfectly prepared to do everything for defence, do not like an aggressive war'. (Buxton to Harcourt, Private & Personal, 12 Sept. 1914, Harcourt Papers).
[45] The best discussion of this is by W. K. Hancock, *Smuts: the Sanguine Years 1870–1919* (Cambridge, 1962), chap. XVIII.
[46] On the rebellion see T. R. H. Davenport, 'The South African Rebellion', *English Historical Review*, LXXVIII (January 1963); and the works cited in the footnotes. See also especially C.O. 551/60 and 61.

clear to Botha that safety of the Union is first and paramount consideration and that we attach no importance to German South West Africa in comparison.[47]

Buxton showed the telegram to Botha and Smuts, who 'very warmly' appreciated the offer and wanted it to remain open. But they preferred 'to rely exclusively on their own forces'.[48] The South African Government, according to Buxton, intended to call for the assistance of Imperial troops 'only in the last resort and in event of rebellion greatly spreading and constituting a grave and growing danger . . .'.[49] 'They evidently fear that the landing of Australians would give rise to racial feeling & [would] be exploited by disaffected [Afrikaners]'.[50] In the event the South Africans managed to cope with the rising without Imperial aid.[51] By the time the Australians reached Ceylon in early November, Botha had the situation under control. Personally commanding his troops, he drove the rebel leaders into South-West Africa. The bulk of the population remained loyal; 'it is especially commendable', Harcourt later wrote, 'that he suppressed the rebellion of the Dutch mainly by Dutch forces'.[52] The generous peace concluded by the British twelve years earlier at Vereeniging now paid its dividends.

The South Africans, especially those of English extraction, believed that the Germans were implicated in the rebellion and

[47] Harcourt to Buxton, Private & personal & most secret, tel. (draft) 23 Oct. 1914, Harcourt Papers. Cypher sent at 3:55 p.m.
[48] Buxton to Harcourt, Private & personal. Most secret, tel., 24 Oct. 1914, Harcourt Papers.
[49] Buxton to Harcourt, Private & Personal, tel. 3 Nov. 1914, Harcourt Papers.
[50] Buxton to Harcourt, Private & personal. Very secret, 9 Nov. 1914, Harcourt Papers.
[51] Harcourt was much relieved. 'I am glad to know', he wrote, 'that they feel themselves able to deal with the internal situation of the Union and I have all along felt that the landing of Australians there would be undesirable from many points of view. . . . It is desirable that the fact of this offer and its refusal should never be made public. Australian Ministers know nothing of it. (Harcourt to Buxton, Secret, Private & Personal, tel. draft, 10 Nov. 1914, Harcourt Papers). 'Of course, I should have telegraphed to you', Harcourt wrote later to the Governor-General of Australia, 'if I had found it necessary in the end to make this diversion, but I did not want to do so unless it was absolutely necessary'. (Harcourt to Ferguson, Private & Personal, 11 Dec. 1914, Novar Papers). The proposed Imperial intervention remained what Harcourt called a 'dead secret'.
[52] Harcourt to Buxton. Private and Personal (copy), 4 Jan. 1915, Harcourt Papers.

that South-West Africa jeopardized the internal security of
their country. According to the *Rand Daily Mail*:

In German South-West Africa were made plans for fomenting civil
war in the Union, for the invasion of its territory, and for the over-
throwing of its elected government. German South-West Africa
supplied men, arms, ammunition and money for the express purpose
of making war upon a community for which it has professed friendship.[53]

In the words of the *Cape Times*:

Even in her oversea possessions, and notably in South-West Africa,
Germany's colonisation has been directed on military lines and with
military intent. She built her railways in Damaraland as an obvious
menace to the Union; her Press, official and semi-official, frequently
spoke with enthusiasm of the great day when the German flag
would wave over all South Africa; her designs on this country were
open and notorious; and as soon as war broke out ... she compounded a plot ... and she set to work by insidious means to undermine and overthrow British authority in South Africa.[54]

In Smuts's view, the Germans used South-West Africa as a base
from which they conducted 'active and disloyal propaganda'
and attempted 'to undermine' British authority. 'Year by year',
according to him, 'German South-West Africa would become
more and more a threatening danger, and an expansive menace
to the security & prosperity of the Union'.[55] According to
Buxton, those views represented the consensus of South African
opinion. But they were difficult to prove. When asked for specific evidence of German intrigue in South Africa, the Colonial
Office could produce little more than an agreement concluded
between the rebel leader, Maritz, and the South-West Africa
Government, whereby South Africa would become an independent state and South-West Africa would acquire Walfisch Bay.
That arrangement was no doubt intended as propaganda
designed to stir up disaffected Afrikaners. To some extent however it backfired. Instead of aiding the revolt, German intervention in South African affairs was denounced by both

[53] 21 Dec. 1914.   [54] 10 July 1915.
[55] Reported in Buxton to Harcourt, 'P. & P. and Secret', 2 Dec. 1914,
Harcourt Papers.
[56] See the minutes in the C.O. 551 series. The agreement was published
in the *Transvaal Leader* and other newspapers on 26 Oct.

nglish and Afrikaner communities. 'In suppressing the rebel-
on', Botha stated in late December 1914, 'the Government
have had the most hearty co-operation of both races. Let us
have the same co-operation in German South-West Africa'.[57]

South African troops invaded South-West Africa on 14
January 1915.[58] The major force attacked Swakopmund, the
principal German port. Advancing inland along the railway,
Botha, commanding 43,000 men, captured Windhoek, the
capital, on 12 May. The occupation of that city, commented
the *Cape Argus*, was 'the greatest blow which has ever been
dealt to the German ambition of world dominance'.[59] The rest
of the campaign consisted merely of rounding up the enemy by
flanking movements in the north. On 9 July the Governor of
the first German colony unconditionally surrendered his force
of 204 officers and 3,166 men. It had been a white man's war
fought between South Africans and Germans for control of a
desert territory larger than Germany. The colony contained a
European population of about 15,000 and an African one
estimated at the time at 80,000. Apart from diamonds, it had
yielded the Germans little in natural resources, and lack of
water had hindered the chief industry of stock raising. In the
words of one South African saying 'Farewell to German West':

> Deutsch West, thou art a land of pests!
> For fleas and flies one never rests.
> E'en now your winds around me revel,
> Thy sand-storms are the very devil!!
> Since first I knew thee, I've been cursed
> With an enduring, mighty thirst.
> But now I'll take a long farewell,
> Thou scorching sun-burnt land of Hell!!![60]

Nevertheless it was one of the very few German colonies where,
in its temperate areas, white men could settle; and therefore
the British press interpreted the conquest as a stunning defeat
for German 'imperialism'. According to *The Times*:

[57] Quoted in the *Rand Daily Mail*, 21 Dec. 1914.
[58] The military operations may be followed in the Smuts 'Union Papers',
Pretoria, and in the C.O. 551 series. The official account is *Union of South
Africa and the Great War, 1914–18* (Pretoria, 1924).
[59] 21 May 1915.
[60] *Queenstown Daily Representative and Free Press*, 20 May 1915.

It is theirs no more. The colony where in a time of weakness and
indecision we suffered Germany to plant her foot has been wrested
from her by the prowess of the Dominion on whose disaffection she
fondly built, and her name disappears from the map of South Africa.
This great result . . . will leave its mark in the history of the world.
. . . So ends with a rare dramatic fitness the history of this first of
German colonies.[61]

So enthusiastically was the campaign greeted that 'Bothaland'
was mooted as a possible new name for the territory.[62]

As in Australasia, the press in South Africa dwelt on the
severity of German colonial rule. 'Germany has not the genius
for Empire building', the *Cape Times* had commented in
November 1914. 'She can only acquire Empire by conquest'.
A few months later the *Cape Argus* observed:

As is well known, the natives of German South-West have no reason
to love the Germans. On the contrary, they retain a bitter memory
of the fiendish treatment which they have been forced to endure. . . .
  The German militarist at his worst is a stupid unteachable brute,
and it was to military men of this stamp rather than to experienced
men of affairs that the delicate task of governing subject races has
been generally entrusted. . . .
  If instead of the unimaginative numbskulls and military pedants—
men devoid alike of any sense of fair play or humanity—Germany
could have commanded the services of men of the type of our own
magistrates in the native territories, who have a sympathetic com-
prehension of the native standpoint, and above all desire to do
justice, the nameless horrors of the war of extermination against
the Herreros would never have disgraced the annals of German
Colonial history. . . . there is a melancholy satisfaction in the fact
that if the necessity of a stern and uncompromising settlement
should strip her of her possessions in Africa, it will be only a just
retribution.[63]

[61] 10 July 1915.
[62] When Smuts led South African troops into German East Africa in
1916, discussion also took place whether that territory should be renamed
after him. To Rhodesia and 'Bothaland' would be added 'Smutsland'. That
proposal however was not generally well received because 'whether his
name lends itself euphoniously to reproduction may be doubted'. (*Shipping
World*, 20 Mar. 1917).
[63] 1 June 1915.

In London the *Standard* hailed 'Botha the Victorious' as the liberator of South-West Africa:

Instead of sending settlers they sent troops and bureaucrats; instead of making willing subjects of the natives they treated them like vermin and wild beasts. The ruthless butchery of the Hereros has no parallel in recent history; and with it all the Germans could not find European colonists to take the vacant lands. . . . . It is a foot of iron that has trampled upon the brazen image of sham imperialism which Germany set up under the Southern Stars.[64]

If the leading articles of newspapers in South Africa and England reflected the public's views, British public opinion within a year after the outbreak of the war had concluded that South-West Africa should not be returned to Germany.

                              *   *   *

The German colonies in West Africa were invaded by French as well as British troops. The latter did most of the fighting; the French in the end got most of the spoils. On 7 August, a week and a half before the British Expeditionary Force landed in France, British manoeuvers commenced against Togoland.[65] Less than three weeks later 200 Germans in the smallest but only self-sufficient German colony surrendered unconditionally before Gold Coast and Dahomey troops. The Germans had blown up the wireless station at Kamina, reputed to have been the second largest in the world. As one Colonial Office official summed up the result of the campaign:

The men on the spot saw the chance, and by a notably rapid concentration and improvisation of volunteer forces of all kinds, destroyed the station in less than 20 days from the outbreak of war, thus breaking the link with the German forces and ships throughout Africa and the Indian and South Atlantic Oceans.[66]

---

[64] 10 July 1915.

[65] For the British commander's 'insubordinate and indiscreet behaviour' in this regard, see Clifford to Harcourt, Confidential, 23 Sept. 1914, C.O. 96/548. Harcourt nevertheless publicly congratulated him for his 'skill and dash' with which he carried out the operations. 'Correspondence relating to the Military Operations in Togoland', Cd. 7872, *Accounts and Papers*, XLVI. The other principal Blue Books on military operations in the German colonies may be found in *ibid.*, XLV.

[66] Minute by J. M. Green, (39794), 16 Oct. 1914, C.O. 96/549. The official history is by F. J. Moberly, *Togoland and the Cameroons* (London, 1931).

The British and French commanders quickly signed a 'provisional' boundary and administrative agreement on 31 August that lasted until the Peace Conference.[67] The British received the capital, Lomé, and control of the railways. Nevertheless from the British point of view the temporary arrangement was unsatisfactory. Vertically splitting the rectangular territory, the boundary divided tribes and gave the larger zone, which contained double the population of the other, to the French. According to the Governor of the Gold Coast, Sir Hugh Clifford, it would be extremely difficult to partition the colony. In October 1914 he explained the difficulties:

No partition of Togoland between the Gold Coast and Dahomey which will result in an approximately even distribution of territory is, I regret to say, possible. . . . no matter how generously each of the two Allied Powers might be disposed to treat the other in the matter of the rectification of frontiers, it is inevitable that whichever of them retains possession of Lomé, and the railway lines which radiate from it, would secure the major part of the advantage, to the exclusion of the other.[68]

The situation remained the same throughout the war. Apart from petty Anglo-French disputes about poll taxes and customs, Togoland did not become an international issue until the Peace Conference. When it did enter into discussion, the colony was mentioned usually as a pawn, a trinket to be used to help buy the French out of places such as their enclaves in India or their share of the New Hebrides. Though the Colonial Office attached importance to getting the better of the French in local administrative issues, the Foreign Office regarded Togoland as trivial compared to issues at stake in the war. In a minute regarding Togoland written in 1916, Grey reprimanded the Colonial Office for their provincial views. His thoughts provide the key to British diplomacy towards West Africa:

The war has to be regarded as a whole & the fact that we hold all German S.W. Africa & are in process of getting German E. Africa

[67] The diplomatic correspondence on this subject is in F.O. 371/1884. According to one Foreign Office official, the local arrangements had been arrived at 'with a sole view to efficiency, and with no political arrière-pensée'. Minute by Lord Eustace Percy, 4 Sept. 1914 (46149), *ibid*. See also minutes in C.O. 96/548–49. A map illustrating the provisional administrative divisions in Togoland and the Cameroons may be found in the *Geographical Journal*, XLVIII (Nov. 1916).

[68] Memorandum by Clifford dated 'October 1914', Harcourt Papers.

& have all German colonies in the Pacific South of Equator puts us in a weak position for bargaining about Cameroons & Togoland.[69]

Towards the Cameroons the Foreign Office and the Colonial Office pursued contradictory policies. As before the war, Grey wanted to make concessions in Africa to strengthen his diplomatic hand in Europe and to prove that Britain did not seek territorial aggrandizement. To him the Cameroons colony was expendable, especially if giving it to the French would offset their suspicion that the British were collecting the colonial spoils while France bore the brunt of the war on the western front. Harcourt on the other hand viewed the Cameroons as economically valuable and strategically indispensable for the security of the Empire.

Duala, the capital and principal port of the Cameroons, fell before Anglo-French forces under the command of a British Brigadier General, Charles Dobell, on 27 September 1914.[70] By the end of the year the northern railway and part of the midland railway, including the Cameroon mountain area, had been captured. The military operations continued until February 1916, at which time the remaining German forces escaped into Spanish Guinea. During this time the British evaluated the importance of the Cameroons and tried to come to terms with the French.

After the capture of Duala, the Governor of Nigeria, Sir Frederick Lugard, sent the following telegram to Harcourt:

After consultation with Dobell and as a result of visit to Duala. . . I advise that it is very important to retain Duala, which is a splendid port. The Senior Naval Officer considers that it would form an impregnable naval fortress and coaling station easily fortified, and if in foreign ownership would be a serious menace to British possessions and South African trade route. . . . The value of machinery, buildings, stores and harbour works captured in an undamaged condition is very great. A large number of the natives speak English and are hostile to French.[71]

[69] Minute by Grey, c. 21 June 1916 (117797); F.O. to C.O., 22 July 1916, F.O. 371/2598.

[70] For the military operations, see Moberly, *Togoland and the Cameroons.*

[71] Lugard to Harcourt, tel., 30 Nov. 1914, C.O. 583/20. See also Margery Perham, *Lugard* (2 vols., London, 1956–60), II, pp. 544–5.

According to Dobell, 'the Power which possesses Duala must necessarily hold the hinterland. It would be unfortunate if Duala were allowed to pass into the possession of a potential enemy'. The Admiralty supported his views:

... the possibilities of Duala as a naval base deserve serious consideration. If a division of the Cameroons is contemplated, my Lords concur that Duala should be retained in British possession. There is no naturally strong British base upon the west coast, whereas France possesses Libreville on the Gaboon; while the geographical position of Duala gives it more strategical importance than most of the other river towns on the African coast. ... The possession by the French of Duala, in addition to ... the Gaboon, would, in case of future hostilities between ourselves and the French, put us in a very disadvantageous position in West Africa, whereas its possession would put us at least on an equality with them.[72]

Apart from the strategic considerations, Duala had a commercial value: from there the British would be able to export rubber and other tropical produce from the interior. Summarizing those views, Harcourt wrote in March 1915: 'what it is essential that we should have is the northern railway (about 80 miles) from Duala to Baré, Mount Cameroon on the coast, which will make a perfect sanatorium for the whole of West Africa; and the town and harbour of Duala, which in enemy hands could easily be made an impregnable and menacing naval base against our West and South African commerce'.[73]

Harcourt did not propose, however, that the British claim all or even half of the Cameroons. 'It might be assumed that we should equitably be entitled to half the Cameroons, but at the most I do not think we should require or could usefully occupy more than one fourth of it'. He wanted to use the British position in the Cameroons and Togoland to extract concessions from the French elsewhere.

We want from France two things—
(a) their share of the Condominium in the New Hebrides;
(b) their small settlement of Jibuti opposite Aden, which controls the mischievous arms traffic to Abyssinia and Central Africa.

[72] Admiralty to C.O., 12 Dec. 1914, quoted in 'Memo. on reasons for the Retention of Duala by Great Britain' by A. J. Harding, 22 Feb. 1916, C.O. 649/9.
[73] Memorandum by Harcourt, 'The Spoils', Secret, 25 Mar. 1915, Harcourt Papers; Asquith Papers.

To obtain these we can offer France—

(c) three-fourths of the Cameroons (instead of one-half), *plus* our half share of Togoland;

(d) or, if we wish to retain all Togoland and acquire Dahomey, we can offer France *all* the Cameroons except Mount Cameroon and Duala, and in such a wide settlement we could throw in the Gambia, which is an object of great desire by the French; but the cession of the Gambia would be very unpopular in this country, and arouse much public and Parliamentary criticism and agitation.

Alternatively we might surrender to France *our* share of the New Hebrides Condominium as compensation, with nearly the whole of the Cameroons, for our possession of Togoland and Dahomey.[74]

Harcourt thus prepared the way for a cross-the-board colonial swap.

In the Cameroons negotiations with the French about the provisional boundary and administration—in which a 'condominium' was mooted and rejected—the Foreign Office at first merely followed the Colonial Office's lead in trying to secure Duala and the northwestern part of the colony.[75] As the campaign drew to a close in February 1916, these negotiations became urgent. An inter-departmental committee composed of representatives of the Foreign Office, Admiralty, Military Intelligence, War Office and Colonial Office met on the 22nd to discuss how best to deal with the French on the question. Before they took their seats, Sir Walter Langley of the Foreign Office announced—much to the consternation of the others present—that the War Council (the group of Ministers charged with the conduct of the war) had sat that morning and had decided 'to give the whole of the Cameroons to the French'.[76]

More precisely, Grey had decided to give the Cameroons to the French. Two days after the War Council meeting he

---

[74] *Ibid.*

[75] These developments are most easily followed by studying the F.O. 371 series.

[76] 'The members [of the Cameroons committee meeting at the Colonial Office], in face of this decision, felt that it was useless for them to proceed with the object of their meeting. It was suggested however, that the French might not want all the Cameroons, and. . . . the meeting broke up'. Colonial Office West African Confidential Print, 11 Jan. 1917, No. 1054, draft and minutes in C.O. 649/9.

recorded the following conversation with Cambon, the French Ambassador. Cambon had told Grey that 'the French Colonial Party were very excited' about the Cameroons.

... Duala was the only possible port for French Central Africa, seeing that the French could not take one of the ports of the Congo. There was really no other outlet for them; whereas we, for our corresponding possessions, had outlets in Nigeria; and Duala was therefore vital to the French. ...
I told M. Cambon that our Colonial feeling was equally excited about Duala, which apparently was the only port of the Cameroons; but the matter had been discussed with the Prime Minister and some of my Colleagues, and we had come to the conclusion that, as the South African Union was already in possession of German South-West Africa, we ought to accept with as little qualification as possible the French proposals [which amounted to a French claim to about nine-tenths of the Cameroons]. ... I wished M. Cambon to know the difficulties that we had had with regard to Duala, and the reasons that had moved us to agree to the French proposal. I mentioned that all occupation of German colonies was provisional till conclusion of peace.[77]

Asquith and Bonar Law (now Colonial Secretary) had acquiesced in Grey's proposal. The French received almost all of the Cameroons.

Harcourt, though he had left the Colonial Office, still followed imperial issues closely. He was outraged, and wrote the following letter to Asquith:

I am aghast at the decision of the War Committee (of which I only became aware yesterday morning) to hand over Duala as well as the rest of the Cameroons to the French. ... It is all the more amazing that no attempt seems to have been made when making to France this tremendous gift, to settle any of the other outstanding questions, such as Togoland, the New Hebrides, and Jibuti. ...
I cannot tell you how strongly I feel upon this matter, and it is for this reason I felt it necessary to write this letter in order to record in permanent form my utter dissent from the decision which has been arrived at without any consultation or concurrence on my part.[78]

[77] Grey to Bertie, No. 155 Confidential (draft), 24 Feb. 1916, F.O. 371/2597. There is some material of marginal interest in this regard in the Grey Papers (F.O. 800/90).
[78] Harcourt to Asquith, Secret (copy), 25 Feb. 1916, Harcourt Papers.

Asquith and Grey contended that the settlement was merely 'provisional'.[79] Harcourt knew this was not so and proved his point by underlining in red ink these lines written in a memorandum by Grey himself: *Duala was regarded as the one thing worth having in the Cameroons. The Government had, however, decided that the French request should be agreed to.* [80] From this time on the permanent staff of the Colonial Office harboured the grudge that the Foreign Office had 'let them down'.[81] Nor were they the only ones who thought that Grey, by giving away the Cameroons, did not pay sufficient attention to colonial affairs. In the words of the Under-Secretary of State for India, Lord Islington: er Grey is allowed a free hand—like in this instance—he will fritt'if away all our bargaining powers before the conclusion of the war, and we shall find ourselves empty handed in our attempts to secure exchanges &c. with our very astute Ally'.[82] The Cameroons, according to Harcourt, was 'nothing less than an Imperial disaster'.[83]

*   *   *

In East Africa the British faced their most arduous colonial campaign. There the German forces possessed the advantages of a vast and difficult terrain, and a brilliant commander, General von Lettow-Vorbeck. Under his leadership the German force remained uncaptured at the end of the war, though by virtue of superior numbers British and Belgian troops eventually occupied the colony.

At the beginning of the war the Belgians in the Congo attracted practically as much British attention as the Germans

[79] Asquith to Harcourt, 26 Feb. 1916; Grey to Harcourt, 28 Feb. 1916, Harcourt Papers.

[80] Cabinet memorandum by Grey dated 'March 1916'. 'Mr. Bonar Law frankly admits to me (and I think Sir Edward Grey agrees) that this is, in fact, a final cession of Duala to the French'. Memorandum by Harcourt, 'The Cameroons', Secret, 1 Mar. 1916, Harcourt Papers.

[81] See the minutes in F.O. 371/2598. One Foreign Office official retorted that 'it is not a matter of the F.O. letting the C.O. down, but of trying to make them see that we are not fighting this war for the expansion of our colonial empire'. (Minute by G. R. Clerk, 20 July 1916, F.O. 371/2598).

[82] Islington to Harcourt, Private, 7 Mar. 1916, Harcourt Papers. Islington had hoped that British concessions in West Africa might induce the French to yield their enclaves in India—'places . . . of no value to France and a constant source of embarrassment to us as constituting havens of refuge for Anarchists and Agitators'.

[83] Harcourt to Asquith, Secret (copy), 25 Feb. 1916, Harcourt Papers.

in East Africa. Confident that the German colony would fall before British troops, the Colonial Office wanted to prevent the Belgians from moving in from the west. 'From a political point of view', Harcourt telegraphed to the High Commissioner of South Africa in September 1914, 'it is eminently undesirable to have Belgians taking part in operations against German colonies in Africa either by themselves or in co-operation with British Forces'.[84] The Foreign Office on the other hand deplored the 'extraordinary jealousy of the Colonial Office of any action by Congo troops beyond the Congo frontier'.[85] The Colonial Office foresaw difficulties in getting the Belgians to evacuate territory occupied by them in East Africa; the Foreign Office foresaw trouble with Belgium and a prolonged East African campaign unless both sides worked together against the Germans. Both views proved to be true.

In the early part of the campaign the British prevented the Belgians from helping to fortify Abercorn, the point in Northern Rhodesia from where it was feared the Germans might attack Katanga; the Foreign Office then asked the Belgians to help protect the Uganda frontier when Uganda troops were needed to defend the railway east of Lake Victoria. The Belgians concurred, thus restricting their potential offensive against the northwest of the German colony—a point that they later brought to the attention of the British. The British themselves, far from being able to launch offensive operations, had their hands full warding off attacks by von Lettow's forces against the Uganda railway. The one major blow against German East Africa during the early months of the war—the Tanga operations conducted by Indian and other Imperial troops of 2–5 November—proved to be what the official history calls 'one of the most notable failures in British military history'.[86] The Tanga manoeuvers, which coincided with the beginning of the Dardanelles campaign, cost the British heavily in men, supplies and

[84] Harcourt to High Commissioner of South Africa, tel. (paraphrase), 22 Sept. 1914, C.O. 537/526.
[85] 'The result of this [Colonial Office] policy can only be the prolongation of the operations against German East Africa & the unnecessary loss of a good many lives'. Minute by R. Sperling, 17 Nov. 1914 (71865), F.O. 371/1882.
[86] Charles Hordern, *Military Operations: East Africa* (2 vols., London 1941—the second vol. has not been published), I, p. 101.

morale. The War Office subsequently took over control of the
East African theatre from the India Office, [87] and maintained a
defensive policy until after the conclusion of the South-West
African campaign. At that time South African troops became
available for use in East Africa.

During the preparation in the winter of 1915–16 for the East
African offensive, the question of Belgian cooperation again
arose. 'Hitherto we have been blowing hot and cold on the
Belgians', observed the Chairman of the Committee of Imperial
Defence on 9 November, 'at one time asking them to help, at
another time discouraging them from doing so. Cooperation
with the Belgians has got to be arranged'.[88] At last fully recognizing the enormity of the task of conquering German East
Africa, the British now welcomed Belgian assistance. But they
wanted all of German East Africa under their control. As
British forces under the command of General Smuts began their
offensive in the northeast of the German colony in March 1916,
the Belgians simultaneously made plans to attack the northwest of the territory from the Congo. Would they eventually
hand over that part of German East Africa to the British?
Smuts doubted it, unless the Belgians received something in
return. The Portuguese might also, Smuts warned, seize some
of the southern part of the colony; they would probably be
equally unwilling to surrender territory occupied by them. In
April Smuts reported that Tombeur, the Belgian commander, had attacked Ruanda, the province in the extreme
northwest, and eventually would reach Muanza, on Lake
Victoria, and Tabora, the communications centre on the central
railway. The British therefore faced the prospect that all of the
northwest of German East Africa might fall into Belgian hands.
Smuts telegraphed:

Their advance will be due to our assistance and to the withdrawal
of German fighting force from that area owing to our military
pressure further east and south.

A similar situation will arise as soon as Portuguese begin to move.
. . . In this way the Belgians and Portuguese will [occupy] peacefully
large portions of enemy territory while the military burden falls

[87] On this point see *ibid.*, chap. VII; also Guinn, *British Strategy and
Politics*, pp. 41–42, and the works cited in his footnotes.
[88] Committee of Imperial Defence, 'Future Operations in East Africa',
Secret, G.-38, 18 Nov. 1915, CAB. 24/1.

almost entirely on us. Must I assume that each Allied Power administers the enemy territory occupied by its army and that three different systems of administration will thus arise? Or will the Allied Governments arrange for the temporary administration of all conquered territory by the British Government?[89]

Bonar Law replied to Grey that he thought it 'very important that we should have control of the whole of German East Africa after the war. . .'.[90] Grey agreed, and applied the same formula he had used with the Japanese in the Pacific and the French in West Africa: all occupation was to be 'provisional'; but in the case of the Belgians he added that 'for the purpose of uniformity & convenience we think the whole administrative control should be in British hands till the end of the war'.[91] The British allowed the Portuguese to administer provisionally a thin slice of southern German East Africa called the Kionga triangle;[92] but they told the Belgians that it would be more administratively convenient if the territory occupied by Belgian troops were placed under British administration.

The Belgians immediately suspected that the British intended to grab all of the spoils. 'I have had considerable difficulty', reported the British Minister to the Belgian Government, 'in removing a suspicion, entertained by the Minister for the Colonies, that in our opinion the Belgians are not fit to have control over natives—an echo of the old "Congo campaign"— & in making clear that H.M.G. & the British military authorities have no arrière pensée, only desiring to introduce uniformity for the obvious advantage of the administration'.[93] The Belgians refused to hand over territory conquered by their troops. By the summer of 1916 they were entrenched in the northwestern part of German East Africa.

The Colonial Office conferred with the Foreign Office about how to deal with the Belgians. The following minute written by Sir Walter Langley, Assistant Under-Secretary, records a conversation he had with H. J. Read of the Colonial Office.

[89] Smuts to Chief of the Imperial General Staff, Secret (copy), 4 Apr. 1916, F.O. 371/2599; see also Secretary of State for War to Smuts, Secret (copy), 24 Apr. 1916, F.O. 371/2599.
[90] Law to Grey, 11 Apr. 1916 (69128), F.O. 371/2599.
[91] Minute by Grey, c. 11 Apr. 1916 (69128), F.O. 371/2599.
[92] See minutes in F.O. 371/2599. This was done merely to adjust the boundary along the natural line of the Rovuma river.
[93] Villiers to Nicholson, Private, 4 May 1916, F.O. 371/2599.

Mr. Read came over from the Colonial Office today to talk about the Belgian Congo. He said that the Belgians are in consequence of the military operations in occupation of a large tract of country between Lake Tanganyika and Lake Victoria. They have assisted in the fighting but the brunt has been borne by our forces whose pressure has drawn the German troops away from the territory in question.

The Colonial Office are not pleased to see the Belgians in possession and I understand that attention has been called to the danger by General Smuts himself. Mr. Read's idea is that we ought, if possible, to find out what the aims of the Belgians are. They might for instance be satisfied by pecuniary assistance for the development of their Colony, to obtain access by rail to Lake Albert where they would eventually join up with our Railway and obtain an outlet for their produce to the East coast, or they might wish for access to the Nile.[94]

As the Belgians approached Tabora in September, it became increasingly urgent for the British to learn whether the Belgians would be content with financial compensation and other advantages in return for handing their captured territory over to the British, or whether they had territorial ambitions in East Africa. The Belgians were asked what they wanted.

They replied in October, pointing out that they had conquered one of the most valuable parts of German East Africa: populous Ruanda and Urundi, rich in cattle and suitable for white settlement; a port on Lake Victoria; the principal port, Ujiji, on Lake Tanganyika; and the western section of the central railway. Nevertheless the Belgians said that they had no territorial aspirations in East Africa. They merely intended to use their assets there to realize ambitions elsewhere, specifically, on the west coast of Africa. They aimed at securing the mouth of the Congo and extending the Belgian coastline by acquiring the Portuguese enclave of Cabinda and the northern province of Angola—which would mean that the British would have to pay the price to the Portuguese, presumably by giving them territory in the south of German East Africa. The Belgians also wanted an indemnity to cover losses incurred by their East African campaign, another indemnity for their release of the central railway and the occupied territory, a boundary rectifica-

<hr>

[94] Minute by Langley, 13 July 1916 (137706), F.O. 371/2599. See also important Colonial Office minutes in C.O. 691/1.

tion in the Kivu region, railway rate concessions and certain modifications of the Berlin Act.[95]

The British rejected these demands out of hand in November 1916. Thereafter the East African negotiations remained suspended until the Peace Conference. Though the Belgians withdrew from Tabora,[96] they remained in occupation of the northwest of the colony. But the British refused to admit that the Belgians had the right to claim their conquered territory, or to receive advantages by evacuating it. In a memorandum presented to the Belgian Government, the Foreign Office stated that the Belgian demands had given rise to 'embarrassment'.

... His Majesty's Government have hitherto refrained from discussing on their behalf or that of others any final territorial rearrangements in Africa. These must be dealt with in the terms of peace, when the latter are considered as a whole, and cannot be settled now apart from what may have been done or proposed in respect of other theatres of the war, or with such careful consideration of their bearing on any other arrangements that may be contemplated as between the Governments of Great Britain and Belgium and the other Allies.

His Majesty's Government, therefore, while taking note of the views expressed by the Belgian Government, receive them under all reserve as to their future attitude towards them.[97]

Harcourt congratulated Grey on his firm stand. 'The Belgian proposals are outrageous & preposterous', he wrote. 'I am glad that you have rejected them, & wish you had done so more

[95] These Belgian ambitions are discussed in detail by W. R. Louis, *Ruanda-Urundi, 1884–1919* (Oxford, 1963), part III.

[96] The Tabora negotiations extended into 1917. On 19 January Walter Long (now Colonial Secretary) wrote to Balfour: 'The real reason of course for our desire to get the Belgians out of Tabora is that it is most important for us to possess the Tabora Province and as much as we can get to the west of it, as the natural connection between German East Africa and the British Protectorates lying on either side of Lake Victoria. The country becomes steadily richer as you go from Tabora towards the boundary of the Belgian Congo, and Uganda in particular badly needs the accession of rich territory which is available in this direction. Unfortunately, however, this is not the kind of reason on which we can dilate in trying to get the Belgians out of Tabora!' (Long to Balfour, 19 Jan. 1917, F.O. 371/2856). Fortunately for the British, the Belgians regarded Tabora as a liability because of its difficult administration and because its occupation overextended their supply lines. They handed it over to the British on 25 February 1917.

[97] F. O. Memorandum, 8 Nov. 1916, F.O. 371/2599.

violently!'[98] Though he caved in to the French in the Cameroons, Grey stood up to the Belgians in East Africa.

*   *   *

By the close of 1916 all of the German colonies except the one in East Africa had surrendered. To the geo-strategists who saw the war as a global as well as a European struggle against German militarism, the successful campaigns against the German colonies seemed to ensure the future security of the Empire. Harcourt was the outstanding representative of that school of thought in 1914–16. Even if Germany at the end of the war were to make gains in Europe, he believed that they would be offset by the loss of her colonial empire. German naval bases and cruisers in the Pacific would be unable to menace Australasian security; and the possibility of Germany ever achieving hegemony in the Far East would be lessened. The elimination of Germany from the African continent he regarded as equally important. In southern Africa British supremacy would be strengthened by the Union's absorption of South-West Africa, or perhaps by offering the German colony to the Portuguese 'in exchange for *all* their territory in *East* Africa'.[99] Even though the French might acquire most of Togoland and the Cameroons, the Germans, at any rate, would not be able to interfere with British communications with the Cape. By gaining East Africa Britain would acquire 'the missing link in the chain of British possessions from the Cape to Cairo'.[1]

Those views generally were not shared by Harcourt's colleagues, or by his successor, Bonar Law. Grey thought the war was being fought to achieve goals of traditional British diplomacy: to prevent one power dominating the continent of Europe and to secure Belgium's liberty. Herbert Samuel (Postmaster-General) believed that the breakup of the Turkish empire had a far greater bearing on Britain's security than the disposal of the German colonies. Moreover:

. . . To strip Germany of her colonies for the benefit of England would leave a permanent feeling of such intense bitterness among the German people as to render such a course impolitic. We have to

[98] Harcourt to Grey, 11 Nov. 1916, F.O. 371/2599.
[99] Harcourt to Buxton (copy), 27 Mar. 1915, Harcourt Papers.
[1] Memorandum by Harcourt, 'The Spoils', 25 Mar. 1915, Harcourt Papers; Asquith Papers.

live in the same world with 70,000,000 Germans, and we should take care to give as little justification as we can for the hatching, ten, twenty, or thirty, years hence, of a German war of revenge. Certain of the German colonies must no doubt be retained for strategic reasons or on account of the interests of our Dominions. But if Great Britain can obtain the compensations, which public opinion will demand, in Mesopotamia and Palestine, and not in German East Africa and West Africa, there is more likelihood of a lasting peace.[2]

Kitchener's views also were more representative of official opinion than Harcourt's: to him the German colonies were insignificant compared with the Middle East, and the Middle East in turn was secondary to Europe. Until his death in June 1916 he vigorously defended the idea that the war would be won or lost in Europe and that the winner would have his choice of the colonial spoils. His attitude reflected the consensus of Cabinet opinion.

If Britain lost the war, or if the struggle ended inconclusively, she might have to yield colonial territories to Germany. Which ones? According to a Foreign Office memorandum written in August 1916:

It is quite conceivable, if not probable, that Germany would ask for the restoration of her colonies as the price of her evacuating France and Belgium; if our reply were that the German colonies which had passed into the possession of our Dominions were beyond recall, Germany might retort in that case by asking for territory, say in Africa, now in the possession of Belgium, France, or Portugal, to indemnify her for the loss of her original possessions.

It would seem somewhat paradoxical to call upon Belgium to cede part of her colonies as compensation for her spoliation in Europe. France, on the other hand, would certainly be indisposed to make a sacrifice for Belgium at the expense of her Congo. Here . . . Great Britain may be confronted with a suggestion that, having escaped invasion, it is incumbent upon her to cede part of her East African possessions.[3]

Faced with such gloomy prospects as those, the Foreign Secretary pressed the Prime Minister to establish an inter-

[2] Memorandum by Samuel, 'Palestine', 11 Mar. 1915, Asquith Papers; CAB. 37/126.
[3] Memorandum by Ralph Paget and W. Tyrrell, 'Suggested Basis for a Territorial Settlement in Europe, Very Secret, G.-78, 7 Aug. 1916, Asquith Papers; CAB. 24/2.

departmental body to clarify Britain's bargaining power. Asquith on 8 August 1916 appointed a 'Territorial Changes Committee' composed of members of the Foreign Office, Colonial Office, India Office, War Office, Admiralty, and Board of Trade.[4] Their report formed the first major effort to define British colonial aims since Harcourt had penned his memorandum on 'The Spoils' in March 1915.

Asquith asked the Territorial Changes Committee to consider 'the question of territorial changes in Africa and elsewhere outside Europe which may be expected to follow as a result of the war'. In Grey's words (which were incorporated into the committee's instructions):

It appears . . . very necessary that His Majesty's Government should have a clear idea of what increase of territory is desirable in the interests of the British Empire, and how much of the territory already taken from the enemy by Great Britain and her Allies can be used (a) for surrender to the Allies as their share and (b) for bargaining with Germany in the event of the Allies being unable to impose their own final peace terms upon Germany.[5]

In the first of four reports, the Committee advised that Australia and New Zealand should retain the German colonies under their control because 'it would be desirable and politic to retain the islands permanently in British occupation'; and they recommended that the Japanese should 'not be disturbed' north of the Equator.

In the circumstances the Committee consider that it would be unnecessary besides being highly impolitic to insist upon evacuation, in view of the bad effect which such action would inevitably have upon the future relations of the two countries.

[4] The members of the Committee were: Sir Louis Mallet (Chairman), Sir W. G. Tyrrell (Foreign Office), G. R. Clerk (Foreign Office), H. J. Read (Colonial Office), C. Strachey (Colonial Office), H. C. M. Lambert (Colonial Office), Sir T. W. Holderness (India Office), Lord Islington (India Office), General G. M. W. Macdonogh (War Office), General F. B. Maurice (War Office), Admiral Sir A. K. Wilson (Admiralty), W. F. Nicholson (Admiralty), Sir H. Llewellyn Smith (Board of Trade), H. Fountain (Board of Trade), P. W. L. Ashley (Board of Trade), Lieutenant-Colonel Sir M. P. A. Hankey (Secretary), and Captain Leo Amery (Assistant Secretary).

[5] First Interim Report of the Sub-Committee on Territorial Changes, Secret, 25 Jan. 1917, CAB. 24/3. See also the C.O. minutes in C.O. 537/990; 537/993; and 537/988.

. . . The future relations of Great Britain and Japan would to a large extent depend upon the issue of the war—which, if favourable to the Allies, would influence Japan in the direction of maintaining good relations with this country, and would render the chances of friction arising out of the Japanese possessions of the islands very remote.[6]

In the second report the Committee expounded the 'military and political' objections to restoring the African colonies to Germany.

It is probable that, if the German Colonies were restored, they would be much more effectively organized from the military point of view. Duala in the Cameroons, and one of the East African ports, would be equipped as powerful submarine bases, and the immunity which we have so far enjoyed in the South Atlantic and Indian Oceans would be at an end. . . .

In East Africa many of the surrendered German Askaris have enlisted in the British forces. To hand back these people to their former masters would be to inflict a severe blow to our reputation for good faith and loyalty. Nor is it possible, in countries where our rule depends to so large an extent on prestige as in Nigeria or British East Africa, to overlook the damaging effect which the retrocession of the German Colonies would have in the eyes of our own native subjects.[7]

In the eyes of this group of military and colonial experts no less than in those of most other Englishmen, there clearly was no contradiction between a humane policy of not handing over the natives to the inhumane Germans, and a policy of boosting British prestige by achieving a dominant military position.

In the case of each colony the Territorial Changes Committee found reasons against restoration to Germany. But if the Allies were unable to impose their will at the peace settlement, the British would attempt generosity at the expense of France by giving back Togoland and the Cameroons. If compelled to yield even more, the Committee favoured the cession of southern German East Africa:

It might . . . be necessary to face the possibility of having to surrender the south-eastern portion of German East Africa including the ports of Lindi and Kilwa, and, if it came to the worst, Dar-es-Salaam. The frontier of the reduced German Colony would in that

[6] *Ibid.*   [7] *Ibid.*, second report, 22 Mar. 1917.

event run north-eastwards from the head of Lake Nyasa and then eastwards to the coast, leaving intact a broad belt of continuous British territory between Rhodesia and British East Africa. Even if the Central Railway could not be retained in its entirety, we should at any rate retain the Usambara line and secure the Uganda Railway from any danger of immediate attack across the frontier. . . . If, however, the Germans were in a position to insist on more, we should at any rate aim at retaining a strip of continuous territory between the present Belgian frontier and a line drawn between Lake Victoria and the head of Lake Nyasa.[8]

Continuous land communication in East Africa thus again emerged as one of the primary British colonial aims to be achieved at all costs. Apart from military advantages, the Committee emphasized that the realization of the Cape to Cairo scheme would enable the British to exploit the mineral and agricultural wealth of tropical Africa—the same vision of the 1880s.

The two concluding reports of the Committee dealt with the complex colonial problems in which Britain found herself embroiled with her Allies, and with the revision of the Berlin Act. Fully aware of the difficulties of global speculation (especially as it was impossible to say at this stage of the war whether France would ultimately acquire Alsace and Lorraine and whether French gains such as those would affect Britain's acquisitions of Cyprus and Egypt), the Committee put forward the following proposal of territorial exchanges with France.

1. French cession of Chandernagore and other Indian dependencies, except Pondicherry, which would be correspondingly enlarged.
2. French cession of Eastern Pacific Islands in return for complete cession of the New Hebrides to France.
3. British cession of the Gambia in return for French Somaliland (including the elimination of French rights in Abyssinia) and abandonment of French treaty rights in Muscat and Zanzibar.
4. Abandonment of British claims in the Cameroons (subject to the rectification of the Nigerian frontier) and the rectification of the Darfur frontier in return for the cession of St. Pierre and Miquelon and the abandonment of the French fishery rights on the treaty shore.

The German colonies had an important bearing on that general proposition. 'We should then still have Togoland in hand as a

[8] *Ibid.*

means of amplifying the above settlement, possibly by the complete elimination of the French from India, or by the acquisition of the New Hebrides'.[9] The British could deal with the colonial claims of the other powers more easily since the issues mainly involved Italian and Belgian taking and British giving. The British were inclined to indulge in that pastime as little as possible. They were willing to make a few boundary rectifications and a possible cession of a small part of British East Africa; they were sceptical that the Italians would view those concessions as 'equitable' compensations for Italy's contribution to the war. The Committee mooted the question of partitioning Abysinnia into spheres of influence, but they were determined to retain control of the drainage area of the Blue Nile. The German colonies played an indirect role in this discussion in the following way. The British had expanded their colonial empire at Germany's expense; the Italians, in accordance with the Treaty of London, demanded 'compensation'. The Territorial Changes Committee found it difficult to see where Italy could be generously compensated without endangering British security, which would be the case if Italy were allowed to have part of the German colony in East Africa. With Belgium future negotiations seemed more easy, provided the Belgians would agree to evacuate German East Africa. In return the British would meet 'in a sympathetic and liberal spirit' Belgium's schemes to acquire the southern bank of the Congo, Cabinda, frontier rectifications, and indemnities.[10] The Committee did not seem to envisage the possibility that Portugal's refusal to cooperate would render Britain's attitude harsh and unyielding towards Belgian claims. They hoped that the Portuguese themselves would be favourably inclined to see their territories developed by British capital. So far as territorial adjustments with the Portuguese were concerned, there was need for caution:

It is doubtful whether the Portuguese Government would or could agree to any arrangement involving an extensive alienation of Portuguese territories or sovereign rights, except possibly for an equivalent territorial *quid pro quo*. They are exceedingly sensitive in this respect, more especially as regards Delagoa Bay. It is understood, in fact, that one of the determinant factors for Portugal's

[9] *Ibid.*, third report, 28 Mar. 1917.   [10] *Ibid.*

active participation in the war was the conviction that military co-operation against the common enemy would render it impossible for a British Government in honour to permit any encroachment on the territorial or sovereign rights of her Ally.[11]

What the British mainly desired in regard to colonial territories not under their own control was not expansion but 'British trade access on reasonable terms to the Equatorial possessions of our Allies'.[12] That traditional consideration guided British policy towards the revision of the Berlin Act at the Peace Conference in the same way it had at the Berlin Conference of 1884–85.

In the dark days of 1916, pessimistic ideas about a future colonial settlement seldom appeared in the press. The 'side shows' in the German colonies were a bright spot in the war. Even in East Africa victory seemed near. The capture of Dar-es-Salaam and the central railway in September, and von Lettow's continued retreat before Smuts's 'sledge hammer blows', stirred expectations that the last of Germany's colonies might fall before 1917. As during the partition of Africa, the idea of the Cape to Cairo route through the eastern part of the continent caught the public's imagination even more than it triggered flights of fantasy of those within the government. The principal advocate of this scheme in public circles was the same African expert who had expounded it so vigorously during the late 1880s, Sir Harry Johnston. As early as October 1914 Johnston had proclaimed that the main British colonial aim of the war was the conquest of German East Africa, which 'to our great and legitimate delight [will] supply at last the missing link in the Imperial Chain from the Cape to Cairo'.[13] In February of the next year he expanded his geo-political ideas in relation to Africa before the Royal Geographical Society. He assumed that Germany would not be left with any colonies, and that this might be the result of the ensuing scramble:

Portugal might allow British Nyasaland to reach the navigable Zambesi. . . . Belgium might exchange the inconvenient strip of Bangweulu territory [in the southern Congo] and the right bank of the Semliki against better access to Lake Albert and the shores of

[11] *Ibid.*   [12] *Ibid.*, fourth report, 17 July 1917.
[13] Sir Harry Johnston, 'The German Colonies', *Edinburgh Review* (Oct. 1914), CCXX, p. 306.

Lake Kivu. ... France would regain all that portion of French
Congo ceded to Germany in 1911, and in addition much of the south
and east of German Cameroon. The northwest of Cameroon ...
would be added to British Nigeria. On the other hand, much of
Togoland might go to France. ... The southern half of German
South-West Africa ... should properly pass to the Union of South
Africa; but the northern half ... might preferably be governed by
the administration of the British South Africa Company. ... Rhodesia at present has no outlet to the sea. ...

He had been generous to the British flag in this suggested redis-
tribution, but he was convinced that our rule was more beneficial
than that of any other Power to the Africans.[14]

During the rest of the war Johnston continued to urge that
Britain should retain most of Germany's colonies and should
consolidate her position in Africa and the Pacific for both
strategic and humanitarian reasons. Those themes also ran
through the works of other publicists, including those by
Evans Lewin, *The Germans and Africa: their Aims on the Dark
Continent and how they acquired their African Colonies*,[15] Albert F.
Calvert, *The German African Empire*[16] and John H. Harris,
Germany's Lost Colonial Empire.[17] The arguments put forward by
those writers supported the tacit conclusion of the Government's first piece of propaganda on the subject:[18] the Germans
were unfit to govern native races.

Only a small minority of pacifists and politicians on the
political left challenged that view. George Lansbury did not
believe that the war should be fought 'to steal other people's
property'.[19] H. N. Brailsford and E. D. Morel pointed out that
Germany's colonial record was being distorted by propaganda.
Morel, the Secretary of the Union of Democratic Control, dis-
tributed war guilt among the powers and believed that future

[14] Reported in *The Times*, 25 Feb. 1915.
[15] London, 1915.　　　[16] London, 1916.　　　[17] London, 1917.
[18] 'German Atrocities and Breaches of the Rules of War in Africa', (July
1916), Cd. 8306, *Accounts and Papers*, XX. See also 'Papers relating to certain
Trials in German South West Africa' (Oct. 1916), Cd. 8371, *ibid.*, XX;
'Reports on Treatment by the Germans of British Prisoners and Natives
in German East Africa', Cd. 8689, *ibid.*, XVIII; 'Report on the Natives
of South-West Africa and their Treatment by Germany', (August 1918),
Cd. 9146, *ibid.*, XVII; and 'Correspondence relating to the Wishes of the
Natives of the German Colonies as to their future Government' (November
1918), Cd. 9210, *ibid.*, XVII.
[19] *New Statesman*, 2 Oct. 1917.

wars could be prevented in large part by neutralizing all tropical dependencies and allowing Germany to trade in the southern hemisphere on equal terms with the Allies. Otherwise, he argued, the elimination of Germany from colonial territories would lead to more wars because of her need for raw materials there. The neutralization of colonial areas, he said, 'would remove three-fifths, possibly four-fifths, of the cause of potential conflicts between States'.[20] But though Morel and others continued to propose ideas such as those, their voices fell on deaf ears. By 1916 the British public was overwhelmingly hostile to the idea of allowing German 'Huns' to participate in colonial affairs. The *Daily Mail* reflected the main stream of opinion when it stated that it was 'not the standard of civilization' that disappeared from the southern hemisphere, 'but the black flag of a nation of spies and criminals'.[21]

[20] In the *Labour Leader*, 20 Jan. 1916.   [21] 9 Sept. 1916.

III. INTERNATIONALIZATION
OR ANNEXATION?
1917–1918

In 1917 the United States' entry into the war and the Russian revolution had a profound impact on the issue of whether or not Germany's colonies should be restored. In its private deliberations the British Government continued to pursue a straightforward annexationist policy; but the public seriously began to consider President Wilson's pleas for a 'peace without annexations' and the Russian revolutionaries' cry for 'no annexations'. If the German colonies were not returned, the Allies would face the charge that the war had been fought for territorial aggrandizement—an ambition almost universally considered to be a cause of war. The alternative to either annexation or restoration, on the other hand, was to relinquish sovereignties and to place *all* colonial territories under an 'international board' or league of nations established in part to prevent rivalry of the great powers in places such as Africa and Asia. 'Imperialism' as a cause of war thus might be eliminated. That proposal was put forward at this time by publicists on the English political left. Their ideas helped to shape the idealistic basis of the mandates system established two years later. In the government the Prime Minister, David Lloyd George, for more expedient reasons, also began to attach importance to a 'disinterested' colonial settlement. To offset the suspicion that Britain had imperialistic ambitions, he 'repeatedly declared' that 'the wishes and interests of the native inhabitants' should be the dominant consideration in the disposal of the German colonies.[1] By proclaiming lofty, humanitarian ideals, the British Government tried to confute Russian criticism of fighting an imperialistic war and seemed to bring its colonial aims more into alignment with the non-annexationist policy of the United States.

Shortly after Lloyd George's advent as Prime Minister in December 1916, President Wilson had asked the belligerent powers to define their war aims. The answering 'note' of the

[1] *War Memoirs of David Lloyd George* (6 vols., London, 1933–36), V, p. 2524.

Allies did not mention the German colonies. The omission caused alarm in the southern Dominions. According to the *Cape Times*: 'if the British Ministry imagined—which we don't for a moment suppose to be the case—that the Union, New Zealand and Australia would consent to give back what they have taken from Germany merely in a spirit of lofty altruism and self-effacement, the British Ministry would be very much mistaken. . . . To restore the Colonies merely in order to demonstrate Britain's disinterestedness, would be an act of gratuitous folly'.[2] In London a spokesman of the New Zealand Government, Sir Joseph Ward (Finance Minister) stated at a public meeting that unless the peace conditions 'provided for the reversion to Great Britain of those territories [the Pacific islands] . . . which had been won by the expenditure of the blood and treasure of the men and the women of Australia and New Zealand, the peoples of these Dominions would never rest content'.[3] In response to outspoken Dominion opinions such as those, the Colonial Secretary, Walter Long, clarified the attitude of the Imperial Government on 31 January by publicly stating that the colonies would never revert to German rule. A large part of them, he said, had been conquered by the Dominions. 'Let no man think that their struggles for these colonies have been in vain. Let no man think that these colonies will ever return to German rule (Cheers). It is impossible. Our Oversea Empire will not tolerate any suggestion of the kind'.[4] At this stage of the war the annexationist attitudes of the southern Dominions continued to guide the policy of the Imperial government in regard to the German colonies—at least towards those conquered by Dominion troops.

The War Cabinet at this time also had to face the renewed annexationist aims of the Japanese. In return for additional naval assistance—desperately needed because of the pending resumption of unrestricted submarine warfare—the Japanese once again demanded that the British support their claim to the German islands north of the Equator. This time the

[2] 17 Jan. 1917.

[3] Massey's speech and the subsequent one by Long are quoted and discussed by Brigadier-General F. G. Stone in the *Saturday Review*, 24 Feb. 1917.

[4] *Ibid.* In Parliament Long was more discreet. See *Parliamentary Debates*, 5th Series, XC, 20 Feb. 1917, c. 1242.

British agreed. The recognition that Japan could not be ousted from those islands lay at the heart of the Anglo-Japanese understanding of February 1917. 'It would be practically impossible to induce her to surrender them', Long cabled to Ferguson on 1 February. 'We should not therefore in fact be giving up anything if we recognized [the] claim of Japan to the Islands'. Despite the 'great difficulty and complexity' of the China problem, the British Government also decided to support Japanese claims in Shantung. In return, of course, the Japanese Government would acknowledge the British Empire's right to acquire the former German possessions south of the Equator. Infinitely more important from the point of view of the Imperial Government and the general conduct of the war, Britain would secure 'additional Japanese light cruisers in [the] South Atlantic to deal with enemy raiders'.[5] The Australian and New Zealand Governments acquiesced.[6] On 2 March Long transmitted to his representatives in the antipodes the text of the agreement relating to the Pacific:

... The Japanese Government have been informed that His Majesty's Government accede with pleasure to the request of the Japanese Government for an assurance that, on the occasion of any peace conference, they will support Japan's claim in regard to the disposal of Germany's rights in Shantung and her possessions in the Islands north of the Equator, it being understood that, in the eventual peace settlement, the Japanese Government will treat Great Britain's claims to the German Islands south of the Equator in the same spirit.[7]

The Anglo-Japanese understanding represents one of the last 'secret agreements' of the First World War. The Imperial Government had been careful to keep the Australians and New Zealanders fully informed of the proceedings which led up to it. As Lord Robert Cecil of the Foreign Office noted later in the

[5] Long to Ferguson, Secret, cablegram, 1 Feb. 1917, Governor-General's Office, 89/216: C.P. 78/23, Commonwealth Archives Office.
[6] On this point see my article, 'Australia and the German Colonies, 1914–1919', *Journal of Modern History*. The account given by Bernard K. Gordon, *New Zealand becomes a Pacific Power* (Chicago, 1960), pp. 48–49, is inaccurate.
[7] Long to Ferguson, Secret (copy), 2 Mar. 1917, Prime Minister's Dept., S.C. 12: 'Disposition of Former German Possessions', Commonwealth Archives Office.

war: 'in 1917, when the Japanese Government were being pressed to accede to the Admiralty's appeal for additional naval assistance, the Governments of the Commonwealth and New Zealand were consulted, and their assent obtained, before the assurance respecting the Pacific Islands north of the Equator was given to the Japanese Government'.[8]

Lloyd George continued the policy of close consultation and cooperation with the Dominions by summoning the Imperial War Conference of March-April 1917. Smuts left East Africa to attend as South Africa's representative; Sir Robert Borden represented Canada; Prime Minister William Massey and his 'Siamese twin' in the coalition government, Sir Joseph Ward, New Zealand. Prime Minister Hughes was in the midst of a political crisis in Australia, and that Dominion remained unrepresented. The Maharajah of Bikanir attended as the principal Indian delegate—an event of unprecedented constitutional importance since India was not a self-governing Dominion and had never before been represented at an Imperial Conference. In the tradition of Conferences before the war, the main purpose was to consider imperial relations and the constitutional problems of the Empire, not the political and strategic ones of the war itself.[9] Those latter questions were considered at a series of meetings of the 'Imperial War Cabinet'—the title given to the War Cabinet sessions attended by Dominion and Indian representatives.[10] At the first meeting of that body on 20 March 1917 Lloyd George emphasized that the problem of the

[8] Memorandum by Cecil, Confidential, 15 Oct. 1918, F.O. 371/3236.
[9] The problem of the German colonies therefore fell outside the scope of the Conference's agenda; but the New Zealand delegates nevertheless insisted on discussing the 'Pacific problem'. They urged that Germany should never be allowed to become a Pacific power again, and that the three Dominions of Canada, Australia and New Zealand 'should join with the United Kingdom itself and provide by some method . . . a satisfactory arrangement for adequate naval protection for the British possessions in the Pacific'. See Imperial War Conference Minutes, Confidential (June 1917), Dominions No. 62. The references to the War Conference proceedings are CAB. 32/1 and 2.
[10] There were thus two series of meetings held during the same period of time: the Imperial Conference, presided over by the Colonial Secretary, discussing such problems as 'temptations of oversea soldiers in London' and making most of their deliberations known to the public; and the Imperial War Cabinet, presided over by the Prime Minister, debating such problems as the German colonies and keeping their conclusions highly secret.

German colonies had to be dealt with as only one of the many problems of the war. 'We shall consider it', he stated, '. . . not merely as members of the same Empire, but also in reference to the great Alliance into which the Dominions as well as ourselves entered when they embarked with us upon this war. The extent to which we can establish permanently our dominion in those colonies must depend very largely upon the measure of success we achieve in the war, because if the success were partial we could not expect our Allies to bear such a very large share of the sacrifice as we who are enjoying practically the whole of the advantage'. Massey retorted that in the southern Pacific, at least, the Germans had been 'very bad neighbours'. 'We have got rid of them, so far as New Zealand is concerned, by taking possession of Samoa—and let me say this, that if we have to give back Samoa and allow the Germans to re-establish themselves in the South Pacific it will be the bitterest pill that the New Zealanders ever had to swallow'. New Zealand and the other southern Dominions were not sympathetic to the suggestion that the Imperial Government might not have its hands free to dispose of the German colonies as it pleased. By encouraging Dominion representatives to participate in War Cabinet proceedings, Lloyd George achieved his political purpose of creating an 'executive' to make decisions for the Empire at large (or at least he succeeded in creating that impression). But by admitting the Dominion Prime Ministers to the innermost circle of the government, he enabled them greatly to strengthen their hold over the German colonies.

In April a committee of the Imperial War Cabinet met to consider 'Territorial Desiderata'. It was a repeat performance of the Territorial Changes Committee, War Cabinet style. Under Asquith the problem of the German colonies had been dealt with by a cumbersome inter-departmental committee for eight months before reaching final conclusions; under Lloyd George the question was resolved at the highest political level in less than two weeks. Curzon presided. The other principal members were Cecil, Long, Austen Chamberlain, Massey, and Smuts. Milner's disciple, Leo Amery, served as secretary. At the first meeting on 17 April Massey and Smuts pleaded a seemingly unanswerable case for the southern Dominions. 'The reason for the very strong feeling in Australia and New Zealand that they (the Pacific islands) should be retained in Britain's possession', Massey said, 'was the danger of the establishment of German naval and aviation bases and wireless stations in the future'. Smuts agreed and proclaimed that 'the retrocession of German South-West Africa was absolutely impossible, even in the contingency of a completely unsatisfactory peace'. He continued:

It would mean the submergence of those who had made every sacrifice on behalf of the Empire in South Africa, and would bring other elements to the front whose predominance would jeopardize the whole position in South Africa. It would give the Germans a political position in the whole of South Africa, and would mean the eventual loss of that Dominion.

Smuts went on to discuss East Africa. Though it 'did not endanger the security of a particular Dominion', it nevertheless 'did very materially concern the safety of the British Empire as a whole'. He 'attached great importance to the securing of continuity of territory by land between British South Africa and British North Africa'. The Committee at its first session decided that it was 'essential' to retain all of German East Africa and rejected the proposal put forward by the Territorial Changes Committee that in particular conditions part of that colony might be returned to the Germans.[11] They reached a firm conclusion about the relative value of East and West Africa: 'if a comparison were instituted between the value, political, strategical, and commercial, of German East Africa as compared with the German colonies in West Africa (i.e. Togoland and the Cameroons) there could be no doubt that the former was of far greater importance'.

At the second meeting of the 'Territorial Desiderata' Com-

[11] 'Lord Robert Cecil asked whether it might be possible to leave Germany a portion of German East Africa, as was contemplated under certain circumstances in . . . Sir L. Mallet's Sub-Committee. General Smuts pointed out that by far the best harbour in the whole of East Africa, and the one which the Germans had, he believed, themselves selected for their future naval base, was at Kilwa-Kiswani, 15 miles south of Kilwa, and this was, in his view, an overwhelmingly strong objection to the cession of the southeastern portion of German East Africa, which was otherwise the least valuable. . . . He was strongly of opinion that, although the Germans would fight hard to retain East Africa, the whole of it should remain a British possession'. Smuts's views carried the Committee. 'Committee of the Imperial War Cabinet on Territorial Desiderata', Secret, 17 Apr. 1917, first meeting, Austen Chamberlain Papers; CAB. 21/77.

mittee Smuts and Chamberlain expanded the argument for retaining German East Africa:

General Smuts from the point of view of South Africa declared that, if it were a choice between keeping German East Africa or the German West African colonies, he considered it much more important to make sure of the safety of the eastern route from South Africa, more particularly as the retention of German East Africa included the provision of a land communication with Egypt, and also secured the Red Sea route to India.

. . . Mr. Chamberlain, agreeing with General Smuts, considered that, while Togoland and the Cameroons should only be given back to Germany under imperative necessity, they were not so absolutely essential as German South-West Africa or East Africa, and might possibly be transferred to the French. It was, however, very desirable, in any bargain we made with the French, that we should put a really high value on what we were giving them.

The Committee concluded that the Cameroons should not be given back to Germany 'under any circumstances except those of imperative necessity', and that in negotiations with France over Togoland 'the utmost importance should be laid on the greatness of the concession made to France, and its provisional character insisted on in order to secure, at the least, the [boundary] modifications specified by the Colonial Office'.[12]

During their further discussions the Committee considered giving the Gambia to France 'for something very substantial in return'; the possible exchange of British Somaliland for Italian Eritrea 'to strengthen the general Imperial position in the East'; and the desirability of acquiring French Somaliland 'in order to check the Arms Traffic'. On 19 April Smuts broached the question of acquiring all or part of Portuguese East Africa. 'It had occurred to the South African Government', he said, 'that an exchange might be arranged by which, in return for the southern part of German East Africa, Portugal might be willing to cede her territory up to the Zambesi, including Delagoa Bay and Beira'. He went on:

With the inclusion of German South-West Africa, this would then give South Africa a natural frontier and round it off as a compact block of sub-tropical territory. He did not think the bargain would be sufficiently attractive to the Portuguese unless it were supplemented by a money consideration.

[12] *Ibid.*, second meeting, 18 Apr. 1917.

Curzon thought it was 'a very big demand' to ask Portugal to surrender Delagoa Bay, 'which was not only of great economic value but an object of Portuguese national pride'. The Foreign Office representative pointed out that one of Portugal's main reasons for entering the war was to gain British support in retaining her colonial territories.

Mr. Long confirmed this view, but stated that he had good reasons for believing that the Portuguese were very anxious to secure financial help for the development of their territories, and might possibly be tempted by a lease on terms, or might give other concessions in return for financial advantages. There was a real danger that if we did not find the money for this purpose the Germans might step in after the war and endeavour in this way to re-establish a position in Africa.[13]

At a later date the committee decided that in future discussions with the Portuguese they should also bear in mind 'the suitability of the Azores as an air base. . .'.[14] Still later they considered even more far reaching territorial adjustments. France might be bought out of the New Hebrides condominium and persuaded to yield their treaty rights in Zanzibar, their enclaves in India and their fishing islands of St. Pierre and Miquelon off the coast of Newfoundland; the United States might cede the Alaskan panhandle for British Honduras or British Guiana; and Denmark might arrange to give Britain first rights to Greenland in case it passed out of Danish hands.[15] The German colonies thus became the basis of a discussion that ranged to the four corners of the earth. Curzon with great understatement at one point in the discussions said that they might be creating the impression 'that we were meditating the carving up of the world to suit our own interests'.[16]

[13] Ibid., third meeting, 19 Apr. 1917.
[14] Ibid., fourth meeting, 23 Apr. 1917.
[15] Ibid., fifth meeting, 28 Apr. 1917.
[16] Ibid., fourth meeting, 23 Apr. 1917. The report of Curzon's committee was discussed at a meeting of the Imperial War Cabinet on 1 May 1917. Lloyd George, though accepting the detailed arguments, did not want his hands tied by specific decisions and managed to get the report accepted in the following terms: 'The Imperial War Cabinet, in accepting the Report of the Committee as an indication of the objects to be sought by the British Representatives at the Peace Conference and of their relative importance, rather than as definite instructions from which they were not intended in any circumstances to depart, notes that the demands of the British Empire

The annexationist recommendations of the Committee on Territorial Desiderata were in line with the main stream of British public opinion at this time. The principal official publicist who concerned himself with the German colonial question was General Smuts. In the spring and summer of 1917 he frequently voiced his thoughts publicly and the press echoed them. He stated before both Houses of Parliament in May:

In the past thirty years you see what has happened. Everywhere on your communications Germany has settled down; everywhere upon your communications of the whole globe you will find a German colony here and there, and the day would have come when your Empire would have been in very great jeopardy from your lines of communication being cut.[17]

His plea to make the Empire secure by ending Germany's colonial empire received widespread attention. In Australia the Melbourne *Age* commented: 'Australia occupies to-day the strongholds in the Pacific which Germany acquired with the exclusive object of eventually invading and subjugating Australia. . . . the German colonies . . . should never again afford Germany the opportunity to menace the Commonwealth and to dominate the Pacific'.[18] In South Africa the *Cape Times* pointed out the danger 'not only to white Africa, but to the whole civilized world, of allowing . . . the German method of using the blacks as mere mercenary war material'.[19] According to the *Times of India*:

The barbarian from the Veldt, as General Smuts styles himself, summed up the position in a sentence when he said that East Africa ensured us land communication from one end of the continent to another and also ensured the sea routes round the Cape and through the Red Sea. . . . With the Germans in East Africa and their line from Dar-es-Salaam to Tanganyika completed, the great central line of communication was perpetually menaced.[20]

An article in the *Daily Mail* asked: 'Why is General Smuts anxious about the future of Equatorial Africa? BECAUSE THE

will require to be correlated at the Conference with those of our Allies'. Henderson, the Labour representative, dissented because 'he was bound to vote against any annexation of territory'. (Imperial War Cabinet Minutes, Secret, 13, 1 May 1917, CAB. 23/40).

[17] J. C. Smuts, *War-time Speeches* (London, 1917), pp. 25–38.
[18] 28 May 1917.   [19] 25 May 1917.   [20] 29 May 1917.

WAR HAS BROUGHT THE SURPRISING REVELATION THAT THE
AFRICAN NEGROES CAN BE TRANSFORMED INTO SOME OF THE
FINEST FIGHTING MATERIAL IN THE WORLD. . . . by means of
naval bases on both sides of Africa they will command the sea
routes to the East and to Australasia AND THEIR MAIN INSTRU-
MENT WILL BE HORDES OF BLACK TROOPS TRAINED AND EQUIPPED
IN TROPICAL AFRICA'.[21] According to *John Bull*:

> Germany has been swept from all the seas; and now it is our solemn
> duty by annexation, by retribution, by indemnity—by every means
> open to the victor—to make certain that never again shall she chal-
> lenge the power of the British Empire, and by challenging it, the
> peace and civilization of the world.[22]

The *Morning Post* perhaps expressed the most frequently mentioned justification for the retention of Germany's colonies when
it proclaimed: 'the national conscience is clear in this matter.
We did not enter the war for gain; but Providence and the
blood of our people have given these Colonies into our keeping'.[23]

*   *   *

A few publicists on the political left dissented from the view
that the colonial aims of the Allies were not inspired by
'imperialism'. Their voices dominated the discussion about the
future of Germany's colonies from the summer to the close of
1917. Norman Angell, H. N. Brailsford, G. Lowes Dickinson,
J. A. Hobson, H. G. Wells and Leonard Woolf discussed whether
the partition and exploitation of colonial territories had helped
to cause the war, and asked whether the future peace in places
such as Africa and Asia might be secured by international safeguards. Arthur Henderson, Ramsay MacDonald, Sydney Webb
and E. D. Morel worked more directly towards a practical
application of the idea of international control over non-
European territories. Their goal was the triumph of self-
determination over imperialism, internationalism over nationalism, free trade over monopoly, freedom over slavery. As with
other idealistic sentiments of the First World War, these ideas
had roots deep in the past. The growth of European nationalism

[21] Article by Lovate Fraser, 'Black Armies: the German Dream', *Daily
Mail*, 4 June 1917.
[22] 2 June 1917.   [23] 30 June 1917.

had spawned the notion of self-determination; the congress system of the early 19th century and the concerted action of the great powers as 'trustees' of peace and order had given rise to the idea of international control; the open-door policy of equal commercial opportunity had created a tradition of free trade; and the anti-slavery crusade had nurtured a sense of responsibility for 'native welfare'. Taken together, those interpretations of history formed the eclectic doctrine known as 'international trusteeship'.

The notion of humanitarian responsibility had the most bearing on the German colonies. By 1917 most Englishmen firmly regarded the Germans as barbarians. They now fought the war not only to restore the European balance of power and to make the world safe for democracy, but also to protect native peoples in Africa and the Pacific from German militarism. So strong was the public indignation at the revelations of German 'colonial atrocities' in places such as South-West Africa that even those who retained a sense of balance and historical perspective did not dare to suggest that Germany's colonies should be restored. Instead they advocated the establishment of an international colonial regime to protect native interests and to allow Germany to trade on an equal footing with the other powers. That particular idea had developed during the course of the war. In 1914 Brailsford, in *The War of Steel and Gold*, had attempted to expose the imperialistic causes of war by discussing, among other things, the 'economic expansion beyond the frontiers of Europe'.[24] Hobson in 1915 published his book *Towards International Government*, in which he urged 'a standing International Council' to regulate the open door in colonial territories.[25] The *New Statesman* in September 1916 pleaded that the German colonies should be held 'in trust for civilization, in order to protect native rights as well as to maintain free trade.[26] Brailsford in May 1917 gave powerful support to the trusteeship idea by stating that there could be

[24] As he wrote in the 1915 edition to Henry Noel Brailsford, *The War of Steel and Gold* (London, 1915), p. 7. For the development of the trusteeship idea during the war, see Henry R. Winkler, *The League of Nations Movement in Great Britain, 1914-1919* (New Brunswick, 1952), chap. VIII.
[25] John A. Hobson, *Towards International Government* (London, 1915), p. 141.
[26] *New Statesman*, 23 Sept. 1916.

'no compromise with Imperialism', and by asking for 'an international charter for the natives'.[27] In the same month Morel demanded 'the internationalization and neutralization' of tropical Africa by strengthening the Berlin Act of 1885, which had been designed to secure free trade and native welfare in the Congo basin. The basis of the future international colonial regime, he said, could be laid by *'an amplification and precision of the purpose of the Berlin Act'*.[28] To summarize the argument as Morel and others had developed it by mid-1917, the strengthening and extension of international control along the lines of the Berlin Act would root out imperialism as a cause of war and would secure free trade. Free trade would allow all nations including Germany to profit from tropical resources and markets, and would enable the native inhabitants to develop economically and politically so that they eventually would be able to 'self-determine' what sort of government and rulers they preferred. Britain and the other powers thus would fulfill their humanitarian responsibility by developing tropical territories for the benefit of the native inhabitants as well as for the world at large.[29]

The publication of Morel's *Africa and the Peace of Europe* in May 1917 clarified the colonial issues of the war as seen from the political left. It precipitated the public debate about a possible international government in tropical Africa. 'The value of Mr. Morel's book', according to the *Nation*, 'lies . . . in its demonstration by reference to the past, how easy and natural is the advance to internationalism in Africa. . .'.[30] Reviewing the book in the *Herald*, Brailsford asked whether Africa would be 'the booty of the Allies or shall it be the cornerstone of an international edifice?' Expanding his views, Morel along with

[27] *The Herald*, 26 May 1917.

[28] E. D. Morel, *Africa and the Peace of Europe* (London, 1917), p. 70. The connection between the Berlin Act and the mandates system is argued by W. R. Louis in 'African Origins of the Mandates Idea', *International Organization*, XIX (Winter 1965). For Morel's boast that he, not President Wilson, first made the proposals that led to the founding of the mandates system, see his introduction to the 1919 edition of *Red Rubber* (London, first edn. 1906).

[29] The development of these ideas during the war thus anticipated the argument developed by Lord Lugard in *The Dual Mandate* (Edinburgh and London, 1929), which guided the development of British colonial theory in the inter-war period.

[30] 30 June 1917.

Henderson, MacDonald and Webb answered that question in a series of speeches in July and August: Africa, they said, should be internationalized in a thorough-going way by the establishment of a 'Super-National authority' designed to neutralize and administer not only the German colonies but all other European dependencies as well. This scheme eventually found formal expression in the Labour Party's 'Memorandum on War Aims' of 28 December 1917. During the preceding six months it was hotly debated both publicly and privately.

The *Morning Post* and its conservative followers refused to see any merit in the idea whatsoever. Even those who held more moderate views pointed out that 'international government' in places such as the Congo and Egypt had been disastrous. By far the most articulate critics of the Labour Party's proposal were Sir Harry Johnston and John H. Harris, the Organizing Secretary of the Anti-Slavery and Aborigines Protection Society.[31] Johnston vehemently denounced 'international interference'. 'Do I agree with the internationalisation of Central Africa?', he once asked. 'Emphatically not. . . . I believe in nationality as I believe in the great value of individuality.'[32] Harris on the other hand supported international measures along the lines

[31] Harris was perhaps the most important non-official publicist concerned with the German colonial issue—mainly because he had the ear of the Foreign Office. So impressed was one of the Assistant Under-Secretaries, Sir Walter Langley, with Harris's ideas about German 'colonial atrocities' that he tried to arrange for him and Mrs. Harris to tour the United States lecturing on the topic. The trip however fell through because, in Harris's words, 'the Colonial Office put a spoke in my wheel with the Foreign Office. They evidently did not want me to go lest I might talk about some of our own shortcomings'. In *Germany's Lost Colonial Empire* he cogently exposed German maladministration, thereby establishing himself as one of the leading propagandists in favour of not returning the colonies. He made several case studies of German administration and in each instance ascertained that the natives had suffered such abominations that they would certainly opt for British rule—a good exercise in the logic of self-determination. (On Harris, see my article in the *Revue belge de Philologie et d'Histoire*, forthcoming). Another publicist, Albert F. Calvert, was a much more prolific author than Harris and during the war wrote a book on each of the German African colonies in addition to a general work on the subject: *The German African Empire* (London, 1916), *South-West Africa* (London, 1915), *German East Africa* (London, 1917), *The Cameroons* (London, 1917) and *Togoland* (London, 1918). Though a powerful and fluent publicist, Calvert was dismissed by colonial experts such as Harris and Johnston as a 'travel book writer' whose superficial works contain many errors of fact and interpretation.

[32] *Manchester Guardian*, 7 July 1917.

of the Berlin Act, but was opposed to international administration. 'Shall I shock you', he wrote to Johnston in September, 'by saying I feel very strongly that there ought to be International *Control* of tropical Dependencies; I agree that the idea of international *Administration* is absolutely rotten'. He went on:

The thing could never work, but surely the effective development of principles laid down at an International Conference on such subjects as the drink, the abolition of slavery, a Bureau for recording statistics of disease, inter-colonial regulations for measures against disease, provide a field for international effort, without any interference with national sovereignty—in that way lies madness. [33]

The Labour group disagreed. 'I am for direct administration, and not merely control', Webb wrote to Harris in October. 'I fully realize the inconveniences of international administration and I do not advocate it. What I want is poles asunder from administration by Joint Commission. The Supernational Authority that I propose would be a single government, not dependent on any other government, and easily able to head off any interferences by any government. . . . mere "control" . . . does not furnish any way out of the dilemma of *either* restoring or annexing the German Colonies'. [34] Harris on the contrary thought that if the German colonies were held 'in trust' they need not be returned. In November he produced his own trusteeship scheme that contained the following points.

1. The basis of Colonial conception, so far as Dependencies are concerned, must be that of Trusteeship and not possession.
2. Existing international obligations should be amended, extended and again accepted by all existing signatory Powers.
3. Obviously Trusteeship precludes national discriminations.
4. Any form of international executive would be fatal.
5. International control or main principles must be upheld by some form of league of nations through the medium of an international Court of Appeal. [35]

The fourth point was the crucial one that divided moderate opinion in favour of international control by sovereign powers from radical opinion in favour of administration by an inter-

[33] Harris to Johnston, 17 Sept. 1917 (copy), Anti-Slavery Society Papers.
[34] Webb to Harris, 6 Oct. 1917, Anti-Slavery Society Papers.
[35] Harris to Garvin, 12 Nov. 1917 (copy), Anti-Slavery Society Papers. Harris was summarizing his article 'Colonial Dependencies', *Contemporary Review* (February 1918), CXIII, pp. 207–12.

national state. Only Webb, MacDonald and Morel—'the real authors of this neutral state in Central Africa'[36]—supported the latter.

The Labour Party on 28 December published its 'Memorandum on War Aims'. It contained the following colonial section:

The British Labour Movement disclaims all sympathy with the imperialist idea that these [colonies] should form the booty of any nation, should be exploited for the profit of the capitalists, or should be used for the promotion of the militarist aims of Governments. . . . it is suggested that the interests of humanity would be best served by the full and frank abandonment by all belligerents of any dreams of an African Empire; the transfer of the present Colonies of the European Powers in Tropical Africa . . . to the proposed Super-National Authority or League of Nations. . . .

Their adminstration under the Legislative Council of that Authority as a single independent African State with its own trained staff, on the principles of (1) taking account, in each locality, of the wishes of the people, when these can be ascertained; (2) protection of the natives against exploitation and oppression and the preservation of their tribal interests; (3) all revenue raised to be expended for the welfare and development of the African State itself; and (4) the permanent neutralisation of this African State and its abstention from participation in international rivalries or any future wars.[37]

The proposal was attacked viciously in the press, most notably by Johnston. In January 1918 he called it 'A Hopeless Proposal'. The well governed and happy natives of British tropical Africa, he said, would be 'de-Britannicised' and transferred to an International Authority which would 'certainly contain cranks and dreamers prepared to ride some foolish library theory to the death. Negro Africa will soon be in revolt against such a proposal; British, Portuguese, South African, French, Italian commerce with Africa will go to pieces; the hundreds of millions we have invested in Tropical Africa (to the enormous

[36] Harris to Graham, 8 Jan. 1918 (copy). Of the three, Harris thought that Morel was mainly responsible: 'At first I was inclined to think that Morel had rendered Africa a serious dis-service when he had rammed this silly proposition down the throats of Ramsay MacDonald and Sidney Webb, but on the whole I am now inclined to the view that this proposal will receive such universal condemnation they will hardly regard Morel as the *only* adviser on African questions in the future'. Harris to Johnston, 3 Jan. 1918 (copy), Anti-Slavery Society Papers.

[37] *Daily Chronicle*, 28 Dec. 1917.

benefit and enrichment of the natives) will be lost, and the British Empire, to avoid financial ruin and starvation, will split up into its component parts'.[38] Faced with such virulent criticism as this, the Labour Party began to modify its scheme. In mid-January Henderson implied a shift from international administration to the sort of international control urged by Harris. At the end of the month H. G. Wells defended the proposal, but emphasized that it now did not include abrogation of sovereignty. The critics of the proposal, he wrote, 'think at once of some new Congo administration and of nondescript police forces commanded by cosmopolitan adventurers'. He continued:

They think of internationalism with greedy Great Powers in the background outside the internationalized area, intriguing to create disorder and mischief with ideas of an ultimate annexation. But I doubt if such nightmares do any justice to the Labour intention.
 . . . Now this I take it is the gist of the Labour proposal. This—and no more than this—is what is intended by the "international control of tropical Africa". *I do not read that phrase as abrogating existing sovereignties in Africa.*[39]

The Labour Party in February formally abandoned the international state project at the Inter-Allied Conference of Labour and Socialist Organizations. 'The idea of a Tropical African Independent Free State', according to Webb, '. . . proved too advanced and too adventurous for this prudent Conference'.[40] In Harris's opinion even the socialists had found the idea so preposterous that 'it has been ridiculed out of court'.[41]

*   *   *

[38] *Daily Chronicle*, 3 Jan. 1918. 'Ahem!', Harris wrote to Johnston, 'This is indeed a slashing article of yours. . . . My exclamation when I read [it] . . . was Bravo! for pluck!' Harris to Johnston, 3 Jan. 1918 (copy), Anti-Slavery Society Papers.
[39] According to Wells the Labour Party's proposal represented the following virtues: 'righteousness, patience, fair play for the black and the common welfare of mankind [which] would wave a new flag, the Sun of Africa. That is my vision of the Labour project. It is something very different I know from the nightmare of an international police of cosmopolitan scoundrels in nondescript uniforms, hastening to loot and ravish his dear Uganda and his beloved Nigeria which distresses the crumpled pillow of Sir Harry Johnston'. *Daily Mail*, 30 Jan. 1918.
[40] *Daily Chronicle*, 25 Feb. 1918.
[41] Harris to Whyte, 2 Feb. 1918 (copy), Anti-Slavery Society Papers.

The Labour Party's agitation against the annexationist aims of the Government occurred during the same time that British troops finally managed to drive von Lettow's forces out of German East Africa into Portuguese territory. On 5 December 1917 *The Times* welcomed BRITISH EAST AFRICA into the Empire. At the close of the year that was one of the few cheerful aspects of the war. The precarious military position in the west and the collapse of the eastern front threatened Allied defeat and with it an adverse European as well as colonial settlement. Even in case of Allied victory there were powerful forces at work at this time against the annexation of the German colonies. In November the Bolsheviks demanded an 'immediate peace without annexations' and published the secret treaties concluded by the Allies earlier in the war. The publicity given to those arrangements strengthened American suspicions that the Allies were fighting the war for selfish purposes. The retention of the German colonies to British eyes might have seemed strategically necessary to maintain the peace of the world; but to American eyes it looked as though British imperialism was at work. Lloyd George's private secretary, Philip Kerr, warned Smuts in December:

It is absolutely fatal to suggest that the German colonies must be retained because they are essential to British communications. The U.S.A. won't look at that for a moment, for this argument leads us at once to the proposition that every coaling station and port in the world must belong to us for the same reason. Personally I am against handing back the colonies, but I am of this opinion because I am sure it is contrary to the best interests both of the inhabitants and of the world that they should be given back to a nation inspired by Prussian ideals. . . .[42]

Later in the same month the Colonial Secretary wrote to the Governor-General of Australia that because of the Labour Party's proposal and the discussion in the press about the secret treaties 'there is a good deal of discussion about the fate of the German colonies'. He went on:

. . . In the United States of America and in Russia there has been from the beginning a very strong feeling against what is called "annexations" and there is at present a failure to appreciate the

[42] Kerr to Smuts, 14 Dec. 1917, Smuts Papers.

difference between annexing territory as a result of victory merely to punish your opponent, and the policy I advocate which is the retention of the Colonies in the interests of good government and the peace of the world.[43]

Like most other Englishmen, Long thought that British annexation would lead to good government and contribute to world peace.

No one more ardently espoused the cause of Britain's civilizing mission and warmly abhorred the idea of an international state than did Lord Curzon. In December 1917 he attacked 'internationalization' as 'a nursery of international quarrel, and the prelude to greater disaster'. Writing with characteristic verve and historical insight, Curzon produced a memorandum on the German colonies that his colleagues regarded as the most powerful statement on the subject written since the outbreak of the war. The crux of Curzon's argument was that Germany had achieved her *Mitteleuropa* ambitions, and at the peace negotiations might thrust her 'tentacles' towards the Middle East and Africa. Since Britain had become the predominant power in those regions, it therefore was incumbent upon her to save the German colonies and Turkish territories 'from a German domination which . . . would presently become a challenge to the universe'. If Germany were to remain the master of Europe, he argued, Britain would have to offset that shift in the balance of power by consolidating British influence in Africa and Asia and upholding the banner of civilization there. To him the themes of British security and native welfare were complementary and inseparable. Re-telling in vivid language the tale of German atrocities in Africa, he predicted the fate of the natives if they were handed over to the Germans:

. . . The long story of calculated savagery and bloodshed connected with the name of Karl Peters, and with the treatment of the Hereros by von Trotha, who massacred that unhappy people by thousands, is no isolated phenomenon. It has been repeated in the present war by the German treatment of the Duala tribe, not in a foreign possession, but in their own colony of the Cameroons, when that territory was invaded by the British and French. The argument is pertinent, because it is to such methods and such men that it is proposed to hand back the German colonies which we have captured, with the

[43] Long to Ferguson, Private and Personal, 28 Dec. 1917, Novar Papers.

added certainty of the fearful vengeance that would be wreaked upon the wretched natives who have aided or abetted our cause. We may be sure that a carnival of blood would be inaugurated in every territory so restored. . . .[44]

He then drove home the supposed military nature of the German colonial movement: '. . . far more than marts, her possessions have been turned into parade grounds for drilling native troops, nests of plotting officials and concealed machine guns, jumping-off grounds for attacks upon neighbours or rivals. They have been not merely a scourge to the native inhabitants, but a pest to the continent as a whole'. Adducing evidence that Germany did not need colonies as a population outlet, Curzon next dealt with the extravagance of German colonial aims and the danger to civilization of a German 'black army'.

For even if we were not driven to counter-measures in the organisa-
tion of an African army, which public opinion in England would be slow to tolerate, we should have inflicted upon Africa the very curse from which it is our avowed object to save Europe, viz., the curse of militarism, naked and unashamed. To such a consummation must the creation of a German Colonial Empire in Africa inevitably lead.[45]

Above all Curzon emphasized the danger to British security which would be brought about by further technological advances in warfare and the existence of German submarine and air bases in the southern hemisphere. 'With the increasing power and range of submarines', he wrote, '. . . the eastern seas will in future be as perilous as the Mediterranean or the Atlantic have been in this war'. To protect not only British but all colonies of peace loving nations, Curzon argued that a 'new Monroe Doctrine' should be declared against Germany. He concluded:

. . . Except in the case of a complete Allied defeat in the war, when the terms would be imposed by the enemy rather than laid down by us, none of the German colonies in Africa should be given back to her, and . . . the Allies, including America, should, in the widest interests of the future peace of the world, be invited to give a unanimous support to this principle. An Africa without Germany

[44] Memorandum by Curzon, 'German and Turkish Territories Captured in the War', Secret, G.-182, 5 Dec. 1917, CAB. 24/4.
[45] Ibid.

will have a chance of developing on the lines of civilised progress. An Africa with Germany will become a cockpit of sanguinary conflicts and pernicious ambitions.

Warding off possible criticisms of his proposal, Curzon commented on the irony of how 'the rescue of a subject people from cruelty and oppression ... is a virtue if achieved by a small people ... [but] a crime if accomplished by a great Empire'.[46]

To prove the purity of British intentions, Lloyd George on 5 January 1918 delivered his famous speech on war aims. Following a draft prepared by Smuts, he denounced capitalistic exploitation of colonial territories and proclaimed the relevance of the self-determination principle to the German colonies:

The governing consideration ... in all these cases must be that the inhabitants should be placed under the control of an administration acceptable to themselves, one of whose main purposes will be to prevent the exploitation for the benefit of European capitalists or governments.

The natives live in their various tribal organizations under Chiefs and Councils who are competent to consult and speak for their tribes and members and thus to represent their wishes and interests in regard to their disposal. The general principle of national self-determination is, therefore, as applicable in their cases as in those of occupied European territories.[47]

Lloyd George's statement was more Wilsonian than the one made by Wilson himself three days later. The fifth of the Fourteen Points read: 'A free, open-minded, and absolutely impartial adjustment of all colonial claims, based upon a

[46] *Ibid.*

[47] Lloyd George, *War Memoirs*, V, p. 2524. The passage quoted above is a slightly modified version of Smuts's draft memorandum on 'War Aims', Secret, G.T.-3180, 3 Jan. 1918, CAB. 24/37/2. Apparently the idea of applying the self-determination principle to the inhabitants of the German colonies had been in Smuts's mind for some time. He had written in May 1917; 'the Russian Socialists are coming round apparently to the view that to the formula "peace without annexations and indemnities" should be added the right of nations to dispose over their own fate. With that I think we can generally agree. And you will see the formula would apply also to the aboriginal population of the German colonies'. (Smuts to Wolstenholme, 29 May 1917, quoted in *Selections from the Smuts Papers*, III, p. 526).

strict observance of the principle that in determining all such questions of sovereignty the interests of the populations concerned must have equal weight with the equitable claims of the government whose title is to be determined'. During the rest of the war the British debated Wilson's meaning.[48] Lloyd George's was clear: the authorities in the colonies would have to produce evidence that the natives somehow would 'self-determine' in favour of the British.

To make sure that the self-determination principle would not miscarry, the Colonial Secretary on 4 January, the day before Lloyd George's speech, had sent secret telegrams to his representatives in the southern Dominions. The British Government, Long stated, was 'firmly convinced that it is necessary for [the] security of [the] Empire after the war [to] retain the German Colonies'; but it would be necessary to provide 'evidence of anxiety of [the] natives' to live under British rule.[49] The nonplussed Governor-Generals of South Africa and New Zealand quickly expressed their great astonishment to the Colonial Office. The former pointed out that in South-West Africa 'thanks to the Germans there are comparatively few natives' to whom to apply the principle and if applied to German inhabitants it would be 'politically disastrous'. The latter stated that the Samoan natives 'have not sufficient training or education to enable them to appreciate and understand the principles for which the Allies are fighting'—though he admitted that the chiefs 'delighted' with British rule might be

---

[48] So also did the Americans themselves. See especially the Cobb-Lippmann memorandum in Harry R. Rudin, *Armistice, 1918* (New Haven, 1944), pp. 414–15.

[49] Four days later Long sent similar telegrams to the Administrator of German East Africa, the Governor-General of Nigeria and the Governor of the Gold Coast. The replies were favourable. In East Africa the Administrator was 'quite opposed to the principle of a plebiscite but, given twelve months of peaceful administration, he had not the slightest doubt that the mass of the people, as opposed to the ex-German minor officials, would infinitely prefer to remain under the protection of the British'. In Togoland 'the desire was universally expressed and with unmistakable emphasis to be under British rule and not given back to Germany'. In the Cameroons there was 'a practically unanimous desire on the part of the people to remain under British rule, and a universal dread of a return of the Germans to the country'. This correspondence is summarized in a Cabinet paper circulated by Long, 15 Oct. 1918, CAB. 24/66. See also minutes in the relevant C.O. files (e.g., C.O. 537/1017) and especially the memoranda on this subject in the Pretoria, Canberra and Wellington archives.

capable of expressing an opinion.[50] The Australian Government held even stronger opinions and instructed the Governor-General to tell the Colonial Office that some of the natives of New Guinea 'can barely understand that the British are now their masters':

While such a policy would be applicable to colonies settled by a white or civilized population such conditions do not obtain in German New Guinea. . . . The native inhabitants number from five hundred thousand to eight hundred thousand, and they consist of different races speaking different languages with numerous tribes constantly at war with each other on the larger islands, so that it can readily be seen how little cohesion may be expected from them. . . .

It would be quite impossible to get anything like a reliable expression of their wishes as regards future Government. Even after three years military occupation by a small British force the natives have a very hazy idea of the state of affairs. . . . To the native mind conquest by another nation means slavery of the conquered or a human feast. . . .

Under all these circumstances it is not difficult to foresee what the result will be if the British Prime Minister's policy is carried out with regard to German New Guinea. . . .[51]

Dismayed at the thought of trying to hold a plebiscite among the head-hunters of New Guinea, and especially sensitive to the American and Japanese positions in the Pacific, the Australians were more alarmed than the New Zealanders or the South Africans at the influence of Wilson's idealism. The peace settlement in the Pacific, wrote J. G. Latham of the Royal Australian Navy (later Chief Justice of Australia), might be determined by humanitarian ideals and 'by considerations which might be described as sentimental, as well as by direct and obvious European interests'. Therefore he suggested that Germany's 'injustice, cruelty, or carelessness of native rights or disregard of native feelings should be ascertained with all possible corro-

[50] Even in Samoa, where the natives seemed to welcome the British as warmly as anywhere, the advisability of holding a plebiscite was doubtful. 'The Samoans resemble children', the Administrator of Samoa wrote to the Governor-General, 'and . . . they act on the impulse of the moment'. Logan to Liverpool, Secret, 31 Jan. 1918, Wellington Archives G. 21/8.
[51] Official Secretary to Governor-General, Secret, 7 Jan. 1918, Prime Minister's Department, S.C. 12, 'Disposition of Former German Possessions' Commonwealth Archives Office.

borative detail'. On the positive side he recommended that 'public expressions of native opinion in favour of the British should be recorded and preserved'.

Where such a favourable result can be relied upon, opportunities for such expressions might be made by tactful officers who understand the native mind and who are acquainted with the leaders of native opinion—in such cases where there is any such thing as native opinion.

If any action be taken upon these lines it is essential that the utmost secrecy should be observed in relation to the various activities mentioned.[52]

Wilsonian idealism along with radical opinion in England thus spurred British politicians, colonial administrators and military experts to establish as a matter of historical record that Britain ruled in the interests of indigenous inhabitants.[53] The Foreign Office's publication of the 'atrocity Blue-Books'—one of which contained photographs of Africans hanged by the Germans[54]—implicitly supported this general view and provided evidence implying that the Germans had committed such atrocious acts that the natives could not help

[52] Minute by J. G. Latham, 'Former German Colonies in the Pacific', Secret, 16 Jan. 1918, Hughes Papers. Latham's superiors enthusiastically endorsed his minute and forwarded it on to the Prime Minister.

[53] From the vantage point of the Pacific, the Australasians thought that the Americans were mainly responsible for advocating the self-determination principle; but the officials in London regarded the Russians as equally guilty of meddling in colonial affairs. In his telegram of 4 January referred to in the text, Long had stated that 'great stress was laid by Russians during recent negotiations with Germans on right of population of country to determine its future, and proposal was made to apply this to German Colonies'. In the press Harris complained that 'now comes the Russian Government, least informed and least experienced among the European Colonial Powers, declaring . . . that the paramount consideration in the destination of these Colonies must be the wishes and interests of the people'. (*Daily News*, 11 Jan. 1918). The same indignation at external interference had led the Territorial Changes Committee to recommend that 'the time has come when it should be laid down as a guiding principle for further action that the only Powers reasonably entitled to a voice in arrangements for the welfare of African natives are those which have territories in the African continent'. Fourth Report, CAB. 24/3.

[54] 'Report on the Natives of South-West Africa and their Treatment by Germany', August 1918, Cd. 9146, *Accounts and Papers*, XVII. For a good example of how the Blue Books were prepared, see C.O. 649/2 and 6, for revised versions of 'Alleged Ill-Treatment of German Subjects Captured in the Cameroons', referred to in the Department as the 'German Atrocities & Lies' Blue Book.

but have a pro-British attitude. The argument of 'self-determination' clearly seemed to work in favour of the British.

The opinion that the inhabitants of the German colonies would prefer British rule reflected the general conviction of the public that there was a fundamental difference between the colonial policies of the two countries. The popular view held that British policy was morally, politically and economically sound, and that German policy was morally indefensible, politically and economically unsound, and criminally brutal. The British therefore had a responsibility to protect the natives from German militarism. In 1917 Cecil had asked in the House of Commons: 'I do not say that we attacked the German African Colonies in order to rescue the native[s] from misgovernment. . . . But, having rescued them, are you to hand them back?'[55] In 1918 the answer of the public continued to be a vociferous and practically unanimous 'no'. Handing the colonies back, even with international safeguards, might enable the Germans to punish or execute the natives who had cooperated with the Allies; and the Germans moreover would then have the human material to build a huge black army to make a future bid for world hegemony. That prospect was especially alarming, particularly if the Allies lost the war or were forced to conclude a negotiated peace. In that event Germany—in return for yielding her islands in the Pacific—might demand the return of her African colonies and an additional block of tropical Africa stretching from the Atlantic to the Indian ocean—a *Mittelafrika*.[56] This gigantic German military base in the middle of Africa would be the opposite of the Labour party's idea of a great independent free State. Far from abolishing imperialism, Germany would become the personification of an imperialistic power by using her African empire as a naval base from which her cruisers and submarines would menace Allied shipping the world over. The Germans would exploit the mineral

---

[55] *Parliamentary Debates*, 5th series, XCIII, c. 1670, 16 May 1917.

[56] There are no satisfactory works on the subject. For a good example of how statements of German publicists could be interpreted as 'war aims', and therefore, from the British point of view, seemed to provide justification for the retention of the German colonies, see memoranda by Curzon, 'German and Turkish Territories Captured in the War', Secret, G.-182, 5 Dec. 1917, CAB. 24/4, and Smuts, 'The German Colonies at the Peace Conference', Secret, P.-25, 11 July 1918, Smuts Papers; CAB. 29/1/3.

and vegetable products of tropical Africa to strengthen their commercial and industrial position in Europe; and they would militarize the natives under their sway eventually to attack the African colonies of other powers. Whatever the truth of those speculations, their reiteration by the press established beyond doubt—at least so far as the British public was concerned—that Britain's colonial rule was beneficent, disinterested and pure in motive if compared with Germany's.

A few weeks after Lloyd George's war aims speech, Smuts in late January 1918 addressed the Royal Geographical Society. Judged by the amount of commentary in the press it was probably the most important speech about the German colonies made during the entire war. Instead of discussing 'self-determination' and 'native welfare', he chose to talk about German colonial aims and the economic and strategic value of tropical Africa. He emphasized the danger of a *Mittelafrika*. 'The Germans', he said, 'are not in search of colonies after the English model. They are not on the look-out for oversea homes for settlers from Germany, and their East African Colonies had no white population to speak of before the war'. He continued:

German colonial aims are really not colonial, but are entirely dominated by far-reaching conceptions of world politics. Not colonies, but military power and strategic positions for exercising world-power in future are her real aims.

Her ultimate objective in Africa is the establishment of a great Central African Empire, comprising not only her Colonies before the war, but also all the English, French, Belgian, and Portuguese possessions south of the Sahara and Lake Chad, and north of the Zambesi River in South Africa. . . .

The civilisation of the African natives and the economic development of the Dark Continent must be subordinated to the most far-reaching schemes of German world-power and world-conquest; the world must be brought into subjection to German militarism and, as in former centuries, so now again the African native must play his part in the new slavery.

A German *Mittelafrika*, Smuts declared, would jeopardize the security of the entire British Empire. Straddling the sea lanes of the Pacific and Indian Oceans, Germany would be able to dominate even South America and Australasia, not to mention South Africa and India. By militarizing the black populations of tropical Africa and exploiting the resources there to increase German power, the Germans, Smuts implied, would endanger western civilization itself.[57]

By conjuring up a German 'black peril', Smuts caught the public's imagination. That speech and the ones he made later in the year were given enormous publicity. His ideas reverberated throughout the British press. The *Express and Star* said that the whole world owed him a debt of gratitude 'for his exposé of the threat to civilization entailed in Germany's colonial plans'.[58] The *Yorkshire Herald* pointed out that Smuts had revealed Germany's plan to use tropical Africa 'simply as a vast plantation to provide raw materials for German factories'.[59] The *Star* gave the gist of Smuts's argument:

A great black army would be planted on the flank of Asia, whose forces would be felt all through the Middle East as far as Persia, and perhaps India.[60]

According to the *Morning Post*:

Let there be no mistake about it: apart from considerations of justice to the native populations, of preserving Africa from the militarism of the Prussian, and of material gain, the return of the German to Africa would involve an invasion of British sea-power which, in self-defence, this country cannot for an instant contemplate.[61]

The periodical *South Africa* stated that fortunately for the natives the Allies had 'blown the flimsy foundation of this mid-Hell Afrika to Atoms'.[62] Most of the press viewed his speech, in the words of the *Sussex Daily News*, as not clashing 'in any way with the declared aims of the Allies, as expressed by Mr. Lloyd George'.[63] The periodical *Town Topics* was outside the mainstream of opinion but perhaps nearer the truth when it stated that Smuts's lecture 'sounds suspiciously like the prelude to a revision of the "No Annexations" stunt'.[64] Throughout the rest of the war the bogey of *Mittelafrika* overshadowed the public's vision of the idealistic colonial goals described by Lloyd George.

*   *   *

[57] Smuts's speech was reported in *The Times* and other newspapers on 29 Jan. 1918.
[58] 29 Jan. 1918.   [59] 30 Jan. 1918.   [60] 29 Jan. 1918
[61] 31 Jan. 1918.   [62] 2 Feb. 1918.   [63] 30 Jan. 1918.
[64] 2 Feb. 1918. For more newspaper opinion, see my article, 'South-West African Origins of the "Sacred Trust"', *African Affairs*, LXVI (January 1967).

The main currents of ideas that flowed through governmental channels in 1918 did not differ fundamentally from those in the press. The depth of discussion was greater because of access to confidential and secret information that could be debated candidly; and the arguments were more sophisticated because of the sustained attention given to the question by experts. But the basic issue of 'annexation or internationalization' was the same. The Colonial Office and the Board of Trade took up the extreme sides of the argument. The former railed against 'what passes as public opinion'—in other words, uninformed editorial comments—and continued to press for annexation of the colonies without compromising double-talk. 'Can we afford to surrender any or all of these [East and West African] . . . Colonies?', one official asked in a Colonial Office memorandum circulated to the War Cabinet in January. He objected to the question itself.

In no country of the world, save our own, would the question be put in this way. It would not be "Why not?" but "Why"? In any other country the opponent would be left to find an answer to "Why?" It would be left to the enemy to explain why—when we have conquered these territories at a very large cost in life and treasure —we should treat these as negligible and hand him back his territories as a *beau geste*.[65]

In that argument the Colonial Office inveighed against a dead issue because no one in governmental circles advocated the restoration of Germany's colonial empire. On the other hand the Board of Trade proposed the live measure of internationalization, which the Colonial Office found almost as objectionable. 'I . . . do not believe that any system of international control is possible, or will bear the smallest real examination', Long wrote in February.[66] Like the *Morning Post*, the Colonial Office tended to regard anything short of complete annexation as a capitulation to the enemies of the Empire. In fact the 'international status' for tropical Africa proposed by the Board of Trade, like the Labour Party's modified scheme, had as its basis merely the Berlin and Brussels Acts:

[65] Memorandum by G. V. Fiddes circulated by Long to the War Cabinet, G.T.-3174, Confidential, 2 Jan. 1918, CAB. 24/37/1 & 2.
[66] Long to Ferguson, Personal and Confidential, 8 Feb. 1918, Novar Papers.

Certainly it would require very strong reasons indeed to induce us to surrender any part of our sovereignty in Africa to a new "Sovereign" State, but this should not prevent us from examining with an open mind the commercial and economic results of maintaining and developing the international system inaugurated by the Berlin and Brussels Acts. . . .

From a purely British trade point of view it will be of much greater value to us to secure an "open door" for a period of years in the French, Belgian and Portuguese Colonies (not to mention the German) than to obtain preferential treatment in British Colonies in Equatorial Africa. From a purely commercial stand point therefore we should welcome a Conventional régime prescribing the "open door".[67]

The 'open door' lay at the heart of an international system which would not only strengthen Britain's commerce but also uphold native rights and contribute to the peaceful development of tropical Africa. To the Board of Trade and Labour Party alike, the traditional British principle of free trade seemed to offer the panacea for the colonial problems of the war.

As the watchdog of British colonial interests, the Colonial Office exerted a far greater influence on British policy towards the German colonies than other departments such as the Board of Trade, the Department of Information, the Admiralty and the India Office. Each of those agencies occasionally ventured comments when some aspect of the issue touched its institutional concern: commerce, propaganda, sea power, and, in the case of the India Office, German East Africa. The Colonial Office dealt with all of those questions and continued its traditional functions of maintaining relations with the self-governing Dominions and administering the colonies, protectorates and other territories under the jurisdiction of the Crown. But the Colonial Office's voice was by no means decisive in the question of the future of Germany's colonies. When the Imperial War Cabinet was not in session, policy towards the German colonies was shaped by the War Cabinet, of which the Colonial Secretary was not a member.[68] He along with the heads of other departments circulated memoranda for the consideration of the War Cabinet;

[67] Board of Trade memorandum by Sir H. Llewellyn Smith circulated to the War Cabinet by A. H. Stanley, G.T.-3313, 11 Jan. 1918, CAB. 24/39.
[68] On this point see Lloyd George, *War Memoirs*, IV, chap. I.

but actual policy regarding this issue was decided by the War Cabinet itself and, to a lesser extent, by the 'Eastern Committee' appointed by Lloyd George in March 1918.[69]

The formation of the Eastern Committee marked an important development in the evolution of the German colonial question. Previously discussed as a more or less isolated aspect of the war, the members of this Committee now studied the issue in relation to the problems of the Middle East and Russia. As in the case of the 'Territorial Desiderata' Committee of the preceding year, Curzon presided. The other members were Balfour, Smuts, Wilson (Chief of the Imperial General Staff), and Montagu (Secretary of State for India). The Committee was appointed at Milner's suggestion at a time when the Germans with renewed offensives threatened to break through on the western front and then, so the British believed, turn to the east. The purpose was to grasp 'the essential inter-connection' of British policies towards the western and eastern fronts.[70] The Committee spent much of its time discussing the problems of the Middle East, which had important ramifications for the issue of the German colonies. In one of the first meetings the Committee analysed the meaning of self-determination. Curzon said that the phrase had been 'increasingly used as a watchword since President Wilson's entry into the war'. Balfour added 'that President Wilson did not seriously mean to apply his formula outside Europe. He meant that no "civilized" communities should remain under the heel of other "civilized" communities: as to politically inarticulate peoples, he would probably not say

[69] Very little has been written on the Eastern Committee, but see Richard H. Ullman, *Intervention and the War* (Princeton, N.J., 1961), p. 307 note 16. After its appointment Milner wrote to Smuts: 'I am hoping that, as you are on the new Eastern Committee, you may have opportunities of waking up the F.O., though under its present headship & sub-headship (Hardinge!!!) it can never be good. But it is at any rate a beginning to get one live man into the business. I don't think Curzon will make a bad Chairman. He is much too slow & pompous & only half-awake to the urgency and critical character of the situation. But if once he can be got going, he *knows* a good deal & is capable of hard work'. (Milner to Smuts, 22 Mar. 1918, Smuts Papers). The quotation is of interest, among other reasons, because before the war Hardinge had assumed a severe attitude towards German colonial activities and during the war the Foreign Secretary, Balfour, was perhaps the Cabinet member most inclined to return some of the German colonies.

[70] See Milner to Lloyd George, Very Confidential (copy), 20 Mar. 1918, Milner Papers.

more than that their true interests should prevail as against exploitation by conquerors'.

In view of American experience in the Philippines, and of the practical impossibility of applying "self-determination" to the German colonies and to the Pacific Islands, it appeared to Mr. Balfour unlikely that President Wilson would oppose the policy suggested.[71]

'The policy suggested' consisted of forgetting that Lloyd George had stated that the principle of self-determination was applicable to the German colonies.

Balfour rejected as absurd the idea of self-determination for territories of Africa and the Pacific. And he did not hesitate to criticize other popular notions—such as the ones that joint administrations in a condominium could never be satisfactory solutions and that to be 'secure' Britain should retain as many of the German colonies as possible. In a pessimistic memorandum written after the Allies' reverses on the western front during the spring of 1918, he argued that the German possessions in West and East Africa should be used as pawns 'to smooth the peace negotiations'. With South-West Africa and the Pacific islands in the hands of the southern Dominions and Japan, the security of the Empire would not be endangered, he argued, unless *Germany* were to regain the other colonies; if Togoland, the Cameroons and German East Africa were parcelled out among France, Belgium and Italy—powers 'bitten with the mania for colonial expansion'—Britain would achieve more easily her goals in such places of more vital importance as the Middle East.[72] In making that proposal he implicitly denied the importance of German East Africa as one of the future hubs of British communication. If colonial issues could be manipulated to secure a stable peace, Balfour, like his uncle Lord Salisbury in the late 1880s, did not mind sacrificing the Cape to Cairo route.

The Colonial Secretary found himself in 'sharp disagreement' with most of Balfour's views. He denounced the Foreign Secretary's idea that Britain should assume the responsibility of satisfying the territorial aspirations of the Allies in Africa. He

[71] Eastern Committe Minutes, Secret, 24 Apr. 1918, CAB. 27/24.
[72] Memorandum by Balfour, Secret, G.T.-4774, 2 May 1918, CAB. 24/53.

objected in particular to the suggestion that German East Africa might be sacrificed 'to France, Italy and Belgium with the object of demonstrating our altruism to the world'. As to the solution of a condominium, he thought it would be 'utterly unworkable in practice'. Long above all deprecated the tone of Balfour's comments about the Dominions, which seemed to suggest:

We, Great Britain, are altruists and desire nothing for ourselves. But our Dominions are different. They desire certain things, and they must have them. We are sorry, but we must therefore obstruct any settlement which would clash with their interests, though we are perfectly willing to sacrifice interests that are purely British.

Long thought it unwise to draw between British and Imperial interests a distinction which might imply that the statesmen of the Dominions 'stand on a lower plane'. 'Before the world the British Empire, and its interests', Long wrote, 'should be one and indivisible'. Far from objecting to the territorial ambitions of the southern Dominions, he thought that their aims 'are absolutely sound from every point of view, are conceived in the best interests of the Empire as a whole, and afford an example which we should do well to follow'.[73] The attitude of Long and his subordinates in the Colonial Office may be summarized by a phrase in the *Morning Post*, 'WE HOLD WHAT WE HAVE'.[74]

The divergence of views between the Foreign Office and Colonial Office had been apparent since the outbreak of the war. Balfour, like Grey, saw the future of the German colonies in the perspective of a peace settlement determined by European issues. Long, like Harcourt, envisaged a settlement shaped in large part by colonial considerations. In the War Cabinet Smuts more than any other member clarified this conflict of opinion about the importance of the German colonies. In July 1918 he resolved the issue in a way that led directly to the British Government's support of the mandates system the following January. First he elucidated the colonial aims of the Germans. At their most extreme, the Germans wanted the return of their tropical African colonies along with Belgian and Portuguese Africa: *Mittelafrika*. For that they would be willing to forfeit their islands in the Pacific and, Smuts hoped,

[73] Memorandum by Long, Secret, G.T.-4816, 11 June 1918, CAB. 24/54.
[74] 16 July 1918.

South-West Africa. He thus overcame the difficulty of Dominion and Japanese claims. But even with the absorption of the colonies in the vicinity of the Dominions, there could be no doubt that Germany in possession of the resources of tropical Africa and in a position to challenge British supremacy at sea would pose the gravest possible danger to the Empire. Therefore the problem consisted of how to prevent Germany from achieving that goal. If the Allies won a decisive victory, Smuts argued that Britain would be able to protect herself in future wars by the acquisition of German East Africa; even if the Germans by submarine warfare gained command of the seas, the British could still hold their empire intact by continuous land and air communication. If on the other hand the war ended indecisively, the problem consisted of how to neutralize tropical Africa, thus preventing Germany from using that region for military purposes. Even with the re-entry of Germany into Africa, Britain might secure herself against aggression by the establishment of what Smuts called a 'Development Board' constituted under international convention. The purpose of this device was the same as the modified Labour Party proposal of the previous February, the main points of which were demilitarization and free trade. Though not as desirable as complete British control over regions strategically vital to the Empire, this solution had the advantage of appealing to President Wilson, who would be impressed with the altruism of British aims. And since the territory under the supervision of this Development Board would presumably include all of tropical Africa, the Portuguese colonies would also be placed under its control. South Africa would thus be protected from German intrigue in places such as Delagoa Bay and the British would be given international justification for intervention in Portuguese Africa in the event of native uprisings or the breakdown of authority caused by revolution in Portugal. International control in tropical Africa would thus foster British security—the primary concern of the War Cabinet.[75] So comprehensively and cogently did Smuts develop his argument that it

[75] Memorandum by Smuts, 'The German Colonies at the Peace Conference', Secret, P.-25, 11 July 1918, Smuts Papers; CAB. 29/1/3. Amery wrote: 'I liked your paper on the German Colonies immensely and I am sure it will do a lot to steady Cabinet opinion'. Amery to Smuts, 16 July 1918, Smuts Papers. See also Hancock, *Smuts*, pp. 498–99.

won even the qualified support of that arch-imperialist, Lord Curzon.[76] After Smuts's contribution of July there was a much greater consensus of War Cabinet opinion on the German colonial question.

When the Imperial War Cabinet reconvened during the Allied offensive on the western front in August, the Prime Ministers of the Dominions debated Smuts's scheme for international control in relation to the role that the United States would play in the colonial settlement. They assumed that the Allies would win a decisive victory. Sir Robert Borden of Canada attached importance to the idealistic side of Smuts's proposal because it might help to persuade Canadians as well as Americans that the British Empire had not fought the war for selfish purposes. He agreed with a statement made by Balfour during a review of war aims that the British 'should try to avoid coming out of this war with accessions of territory compared with which those of other States would sink into insignificance'.[77] According to Borden, it would be disastrous to create the impression that the war had been fought to extend the frontiers of the Empire. To avoid this he thought that the Americans should be allowed to take over some of the conquered territory:

The more it was possible to get the United States to undertake responsibility in world affairs, the better for the world as a whole and for the British Empire. For his own part, speaking of the German Colonies generally, and not dealing with the specific interests which other Dominions might have with respect to some of them, he would be perfectly ready to let any of these Colonies pass under the direct protectorate or even the real ownership and control of the United States. The real difficulty would be the reluctance of the Americans themselves to depart from their historic policy.[78]

[76] Memorandum by Curzon, Secret, G.-218, 25 July 1918, CAB. 24/5.
[77] War Cabinet Minutes, Secret, 457, 13 Aug. 1918, CAB. 23/7.
[78] Ibid. Nevertheless the idea of the United States assuming colonial responsibilities was alive in American circles. Wilson's colonial adviser, G. L. Beer, wanted the United States to take over the Cameroons: 'Possibly the most advantageous areas for such an experiment would be the Cameroons and Asiatic Turkey exclusive of Irak. The only objection that I can see is that we would probably spend so much money in developing West Africa that the other colonizing Powers could not stand the pace'. (Beer to Curtis, copy, 11 July 1918, Lothian Papers). See my article, 'The United States and the African Peace Settlement of 1919: the Pilgrimage of George Louis Beer', Journal of African History, IV (1963).

Massey and Hughes on the other hand doubted whether the United States should be offered any colonial territory, especially in the Pacific. Massey said that he was not prepared 'to agree to the idea that America should be given any of the Pacific Islands which we had conquered', and that nothing other than British annexation would be satisfactory. Hughes's attitude was that 'as regards the Pacific islands . . . if anyone wanted to shift Australia from them they would have to come and do it!'[79] No one suggested that South-West Africa might be given to the Americans or, at this stage, even placed under international control. The discussion therefore narrowed itself to the future of Togoland, the Cameroons and German East Africa. Lloyd George thought that 'if we approached the United States with a view to their undertaking the responsibilities of trusteeship, say for Palestine and one of the German African Colonies, they might be prepared to recognize our trusteeship elsewhere, as for instance in Mesopotamia'. Smuts argued that his scheme of a Development Board would eliminate territorial difficulties. 'Our principal trouble', he said, 'would be with the United States, and it would be essential to conciliate them by bringing them into the business. . . . While we should retain the German Colonies territorially, the whole of tropical Africa should be placed under a Development Board, the Presidency of which should be entrusted to the United States'.[80] In that way Wilson might be more prepared to uphold specific British claims. Gaining the support of the United States—'playing up to America and moving her on to back us up', as Smuts later put it to the Eastern Committee[81]—became the dominant concern of British statesmen involved in colonial questions during the last months of the war.

[79] War Cabinet Minutes, Secret, 458, 14 Aug. 1918, CAB. 23/7.
[80] 'A certain amount of discussion followed as to the precise scope and powers of such a Development Board and of its relations to the actual territorial Sovereign. It was pointed out that the scheme was susceptible of immense modifications according as practically all the powers were given to the Board and territorial sovereignty limited to police duties, or the Board confined to the mere overseeing of the carrying out of certain treaty restrictions. It was also pointed out that the other colonial Powers affected might object to such a Board, most of all, perhaps, a Power like Portugal, in whose case external control was most desirable'. *Ibid.*
[81] Eastern Committee Minutes, Secret, 2 Dec. 1918, CAB. 27/24.

The idea of an Anglo-American 'colonial understanding'[82] rested on the assumption that the Americans would be willing to assume some sort of responsibility for the administration in one or more of the former German or Turkish territories. Though some members of the Imperial War Cabinet doubted that Wilson would consent to involvement in European colonial affairs, all agreed that it would be desirable at least to be able to make an offer to take over a 'burden' of 'first-class importance'. Where? The two most frequently mentioned territories were German East Africa and Palestine. Opinion about which one was more suitable divided between those who thought that the Middle East was more strategically important to the Empire than tropical Africa, and those who thought the opposite. To those such as Curzon who held that both regions were strategically valuable, that choice posed a dilemma. Curzon solved it by arguing that the United States should take over territories not under British sway. He thought that the parts of tropical Africa and the Middle East already in contact with British culture would suffer if given to another power, and that American ambitions in that part of the world should not be encouraged.

Speaking for himself, with a life's experience of seeing the work done by England in the development of backward countries, he [Curzon] saw no reason why we should be so urgent in handing over such a region [German East Africa] to anybody else. While entirely in favour of the idea of the United States extending its responsibilities where it could properly do so, he was not otherwise anxious to set up a series of American colonies everywhere in proximity to ours. . . .[83]

In a series of vigorously written memoranda and letters to members of the Imperial War Cabinet, Amery supported Curzon's point of view and urged, among other things, that the United States should develop the Belgian Congo and Portuguese Africa.

[82] For this idea see especially Gaddis Smith, 'The British Government and the Disposition of the German Colonies in Africa', in *Imperial Rivalry and Colonial Rule*.

[83] War Cabinet Minutes, Secret, 459, 15 Aug. 1918, CAB. 23/7.

I am all for bringing America into world politics. But it must be on natural lines as the outcome of her operations during this war. . . . To dump the Americans with their vigorous but crude ways into the middle of a problem like that of Palestine so closely connected with adjoining territories would be bound to lead to friction, just as it would lead to friction if we, even on American invitation, undertook the guardianship of Mexico or Guatemala. The great thing to aim at is a compact, continuous, easily defended and easily developed British Empire with the fewest friction surfaces with other Powers. If I had to give up territories it would not be Palestine or German East Africa but things like British Guiana, British Honduras, the Gambia, the Gold Coast, or even Gibraltar. . . .

It would be far better for Africa that the United States should take in hand the development of a great central and south-western block composed of the Belgian Congo and Angola, that France should take over the Cameroons and Togoland and that we should develop a compact region in East Africa, than that Africa should be cut up into a number of disconnected minor colonial territories. From the point of view of British security continuous territory along the whole length of Africa from north to south would, of course, be a matter of the very greatest importance.[84]

Given the choice of handing over Palestine or German East Africa to the Americans, Lloyd George preferred to keep Palestine because of its value as a 'strategical buffer'. That prospect filled those dedicated to the Cape to Cairo scheme with dismay. 'We shall have to work hard', Amery wrote to Smuts a few days before the Armistice, 'if we are to prevent the Prime Minister giving away East Africa to the Americans'.[85]

East Africa at the close of the war was the only former German possession whose future remained uncertain. The southern Dominions and Japan clearly would absorb the colonies in their vicinity; France seemed destined to acquire most of

[84] Amery to Smuts, 16 Aug. 1918, enclosing memorandum, 'United States and British War Aims', Smuts Papers. See also especially Amery to Borden, 25 Sept. 1918, Borden Papers (National Archives of Canada); also L. S. Amery, *My Political Life* (3 vols., London, 1953–55), II, pp. 160–61.

[85] 'I am sure if we are to give them something, it would much better be something on the American continent like British Honduras or British Guiana, or in West Africa like Togoland, than break up the continuity of British East Africa. If you once put them there, it won't be many years before they have swallowed Portuguese East and I don't think that would suit any of us'. Amery to Smuts, 1 Nov. 1918, Smuts Papers.

the German territory in equatorial West Africa. The fate of German East Africa was less clear. The Imperial War Cabinet in an academic atmosphere considered giving it to the United States as a 'mandate'—the term that became current during the last months of the war. More seriously they pondered the problem of Belgian occupation of the northern part of the colony. According to the Colonial Office the situation had been intolerable since 1916. The British Government continued to refuse to accept the Belgian view that the East African territory under Belgian occupation was 'definitely at their disposal for the purpose of negotiations'. The Colonial Office gave these reasons:

1. because the successful invasion of the north-west of German East Africa by the Belgians was only made possible by British assistance and as the result of British efforts;
2. because the Belgian view was contrary to the agreement by which all conquered territory was to be held for disposal in the peace negotiations;
3. because there are reasons specially affecting the future of British rule in East Africa which made it imperative to avoid any recognition such as the Belgians sought of their position in the territory occupied by them. (Among these reasons are:—(i) the difficulty of administering German East Africa without the north-west provinces, which form an integral part of the German Protectorate, (ii) the necessity of maintaining our land communications between the south and the north (Uganda and the Sudan) on the one hand, and between the east and the west (the Indian Ocean to Lake Tanganyika) on the other, (iii) the importance of our sharing equally with the Belgian Congo the control over Lake Tanganyika and the communications on the lake).[86]

The British followed a policy of 'complete freedom of action'— a euphemistic phrase meaning that they had no policy at all. Unless the Belgians could be given something substantial, the British faced the prospect that the part of German East Africa considered vital for the Cape to Cairo route would pass permanently into Belgian hands.

German East Africa also entered into War Cabinet discussions as a possible 'Colony for India'. In July the Secretary of

[86] Colonial Office Confidential Print, African No. 1066, 'Belgian Occupied Territory in German East Africa', 27 Oct. 1918.

State for India, E. S. Montagu, had circulated a memorandum
written by an officer who had served in East Africa, Sir Theo-
dore Morison. Morison drew attention to the resentment felt
by Indians because they were not allowed to emigrate freely
to the Dominions. 'German East Africa', he argued, 'is a country
so vast, so suitable for Indian colonisation and potentially so
rich that India may be well content to accept it as compensation for her exclusion from the Dominions'. He thought that
the Indians were well suited to 'clear the African jungle [and
to] build villages', and that East Africa developed by India
could become a great food producing area. Above all, he continued, the Indians would be given 'a higher status in the Empire' and would have a chance 'to become a colonising power
and to play a part in civilising the wild; if I may use a phrase
which they have little reason to love, they are called to share the
white man's burden'.[87] Montagu enthusiastically supported
those views and in October deplored that Morison's memorandum had 'not produced the slightest effect'.[88] He emphasized
that India was 'a congested country' and that German East
Africa would be a good place for Indian soldiers who had
served in the war to acquire land. Montagu's rebuke to the
War Cabinet for ignoring such a 'serious' question received a
scathing reply from Curzon. He challenged the premise of the
argument, that India needed an outlet for excess population.
'I submit', Curzon wrote, '... that the first call upon Indian man-
hood and Indian patriotism is not Africa, but India itself... '.
He went on:

... I ask the question whether India either aspires to be or is qualified to become a colonising Power. I cannot recall, when I knew it,
any such demand put forward by her spokesmen. If they have changed their views, I would still urge that the exploitation of their own
country—the industrial surface of which has barely been scratched—
affords a better scope for an awakening national consciousness than
experiments in another and alien atmosphere. As to the capacity

[87] Memorandum by Morison, 'A Colony for India', (dated July 1918),
circulated by Montagu to the War Cabinet, Secret, G.T.-5132, 16 July
1918, CAB. 24/38. See also Morison's article in *The Times*, 24 Aug. 1918,
and the leading article on the subject. For earlier discussions see the 'German
East Africa' series begun in July 1916, C.O. 691.
[88] Memorandum by Montagu, Secret, G.T.-6028, 18 Oct. 1918, CAB.
24/67.

of India for colonisation on a considerable scale (apart from petty trading and contract labour), that remains quite untested.[89]

The constitutional and administrative difficulties would be enormous. Could India, not yet self-governing, govern a mandate? No one answered that question. German East Africa was never seriously considered as a 'colony' for India. Colonel R. Meinertzhagen, who had served in the East African campaign and who became one of the colonial experts at the Peace Conference, probably touched upon one of the reasons— prejudice against Indians—as he described his own bias in his diary: 'It would be difficult to conceive a more disastrous policy [of giving German East Africa to India].... The experience of the Indian in Africa has been an unhappy one. It has been the history of vice, crime, unrest and general political intrigue; he has been unpopular with the local governments concerned, with the white settlers and with the Africans, and God help the natives of German East if the Indian Government becomes its mandatory power'.[90]

At the time of the Armistice in November the impact of Wilsonian idealism to British eyes was more noticeable in the case of German East Africa than in that of any other former German possession. The Secretary of State for India urged that the colony should be 'held in trusteeship' by India; the Prime Minister proclaimed that he was willing to give it to the United States as a mandate so that the Americans might share the 'white man's burden'. Like Gladstone, Lloyd George did not accept the logic that East Africa should form one of the strategic lynchpins of Britain's Empire in Africa. At the same time he did not deny that if the United States refused to take over German East Africa, the responsibility for its administration would fall upon Britain. Therein lay the ingenuity of Lloyd George's position. There were no positive indications that Wilson wanted the United States to become an East African power. In the words of the Colonial Secretary: 'It is now quite

[89] Memorandum by Curzon, 'The Indians and German East Africa', Confidential, G.T.-6062, 19 Oct. 1918, CAB. 24/67. See also memorandum by Long, 'The Indians and German East Africa', 14 Nov. 1918, C.O. 537/1017. Long supported Curzon's view and added that 'the scheme is causing great uneasiness among the white community in British East Africa ...'.

[90] R. Meinertzhagen, *Army Diary* (London, 1960), pp. 248–49.

definitely held that, whatever happens, these Colonies can never be returned to Germany, and it follows as an almost inevitable corollary that in the absence of any definite proposal for their possession they should remain with us'.[91] That general conclusion was shared by the press. Whatever line Wilson might take in the peace negotiations, it was clear, as the periodical *African World* put it, that *'Germania africana delenda est'*.[92] The same principle of course held true in the Pacific. The war had destroyed Germany's colonial empire; the territories under British occupation would pass under some form of British control. Despite the lip service paid to the idealism of President Wilson and the important concessions such as the possible surrender of German East Africa which a few British statesmen were prepared to make, British policy generally aimed at securing the Imperial lines of communication. That meant the retention of as many German colonies as possible. As Smuts summed up the problem of the German colonies in its broad perspective at the close of the war:

As far as the British Empire is concerned we have practically won and hold all that we want for the future complete mastery of the seas and access to raw materials, security of our communications through possession of the German Colonies, and protection of our routes to Asia through the secure possession of Egypt, Arabia, Palestine and Mesopotamia. To these we must hold as grimly as possible. . . .[93]

[91] Long to Ferguson, Private and Personal, 7 Nov. 1918, Novar Papers.
[92] 2 Nov. 1918.
[93] Memorandum by Smuts, 'A Note on the Early Conclusion of Peace' ('For the King and War Cabinet only'), Secret, G.T.-6091, 24 Oct. 1918, CAB. 24/67.

IV. MANDATES
1919

ON the eve of the Paris Peace Conference the British Government decided in principle to accept the proposal for a 'mandates system'. The reasons for that decision were complex. In former wars Britain like other powers when victorious had pursued the straightforward procedure of acquiring territories believed to have strategic or commercial importance. Those considerations weighed no less heavily in the deliberations of the British statesmen at the end of the First World War than at the close of the Napoleonic wars. But since 1917 the urge for simple territorial aggrandizement increasingly had been checked by the popular belief that 'imperialism' was a cause of war and that rivalry of the great powers in Africa, the Middle East and Asia jeopardized the peace of the world. President Wilson championed that point of view. He was convinced that a just peace was one without annexations. Nevertheless he doubted whether Germany's colonies should be restored. He believed that the Germans had forfeited their moral right as colonial rulers; he thought that the elimination of Germany from colonial affairs would contribute towards a stable world; and he recognized that the Allied powers would never permit the return of the German colonies. He urged that the former Turkish and German possessions should be administered as a 'sacred trust of civilization' under the League of Nations.[1] By accepting mandates the British seemed to bring their aims into harmony with the non-annexationist policy of the United States.

[1] On Wilson's view towards the colonial aims of the European powers, I have profited from reading Arthur Walworth's draft chapter on the mandates in *The United States at the Paris Peace Conference* (forthcoming). I have also greatly benefited from another essay, Gaddis Smith, 'The British Government and the Disposition of the German Colonies in Africa, 1914–1918' in *Imperial Rivalry and Colonial Rule*, which is especially valuable for American policy towards the German colonial question. See also George Curry, 'Woodrow Wilson, Jan Smuts, and the Versailles Settlement', *American Historical Review*, LXVI (July 1961). On Wilson's advisory staff, see Lawrence E. Gelfand, *The Inquiry: American Preparations for Peace, 1917–1919* (New Haven and London, 1963); and W. R. Louis, 'The United States and the African Peace Settlement of 1919: the Pilgrimage of George Louis Beer', *Journal of African History*, IV (1963).

Wilson himself did not define precisely the meaning of mandatory obligations. During the time between the conclusion of the Armistice in November 1918 and the beginning of the Peace Conference in January of the following year, British statesmen and publicists tried to anticipate what Wilson had in mind. They continued to debate whether the German colonies should be placed under international control and, if so, on what terms. The Colonial Office circulated to the War Cabinet a lengthy memorandum purporting to prove that 'internationalism' in the form of the Berlin and Brussels Acts—the most frequently mentioned antecedents of the mandates system—rested 'on a very slender foundation'. 'The Berlin Act', Long wrote, 'furnishes but cold comfort to the internationalists, and our experience of the working of the Brussels Act has hardly been more encouraging'.[2] He concluded:

In fact, internationalism in a mild form [i.e., the Berlin and Brussels Acts], and assisted by humanitarian considerations, has proved, on the whole, a dismal failure in Tropical Africa, and neither past experience nor the logic of things gives any ground for anticipating better results from a more developed form of the régime. I could be no party to any arrangements of the kind proposed, which in my judgment would paralyze our administrations in Tropical Africa. . . .[3]

The conservative press shared the Colonial Office's distaste for international control. According to the *Spectator*:

Colonies are like children, and a child will never develop or be happily and successfully brought up by a committee instead of by a parent or an adopted parent. Internationalism was tried in the case of the Congo, with results which no one desires to see repeated. Tropical colonies placed like East Africa and New Guinea can never become independent, self-governing States. Colonies require sacrifices, and very considerable sacrifices, and these will never be made by an International Board.[4]

[2] Memorandum by Long 'Internationalism and Equatorial Africa', Secret, G.T.-6333, 16 Nov. 1918, CAB. 24/70. See also C.O. 537/1013.
[3] *Ibid.*
[4] 2 Nov. 1918. Along these lines see also especially various articles by Sir Harry Johnston, who should have known better when he described the Congo regime as an 'international government': 'So far as International Government is concerned . . . I condemn it uncompromisingly. We have seen what it was in . . . the twenty-five years of the Independent State of the Congo'. *Cambridge Magazine*, 16 Nov. 1918.

Moderate opinion, however, increasingly tended to support the idea of international safeguards for colonial dependencies. The *Round Table*, the journal which Lord Milner once described as the organ of 'enlightened British imperialism', argued that international control had failed in the past only because there had been no enforcing authority by a League of Nations. Within the government Smuts gave powerful support to the practical application of the scheme by supervising the preparation of the 'brief'[5]—in fact it was mainly an indictment against German colonial administration—about the German colonies to be used at the Peace Conference. In November he transmitted that document to Long together with a letter in which he made it clear that the War Cabinet if necessary would override the Colonial Office's objection to 'internationalism' and gave the reasons for doing so: 'unconditional annexation of the German Colonies', Smuts wrote, 'should be pressed for to the utmost'. He continued that if this pressure failed:

we should continue to hold them subject to the control of the League of Nations in regard to certain specified subjects (liquor, arms, military training, fortification, etc.). Such control should be laid down in an Act of a general character, so that the French and others are bound in the same way as ourselves. You will see there is here nothing . . . about joint control, and a small concession is made about the League of Nations which might have the effect of securing the support of the United States to our holding onto these Colonies if our other lines of argument fail.

Our Delegates will, of course, not make this concession until it becomes necessary to carry President Wilson with them.[6]

Those tactics were exactly the ones used by the British Delegates at the Peace Conference.

When the Eastern Committee in December 1918 considered the question of mandatory rule, Smuts expanded his ideas about American participation. He thought the United States should share world-wide responsibilities in order to counterbalance French power. As Germany disappeared as Britain's European enemy, France re-emerged as her old colonial rival.[7] Smuts said:

[5] Memorandum by Sir Erle Richards, 'German Colonies', Secret, P.-34, dated December 1918, CAB. 29/1/3.

[6] Smuts to Long (copy), 28 Nov. 1918, Smuts Papers.

[7] Curzon's remarks are especially interesting in this regard: 'A good deal

With Germany practically wiped off for a generation we must deal with France. France is a great military Power. We know the character of French policy in the past, and what it may be in the coming generation again. France may be our great problem, and therefore it seems to me that we must try and make friends with America. That is the line of policy for us to pursue. . . . America has no selfish objects at this juncture; America is not out for anything except for the larger issue of world settlement, depending upon the League of Nations. . . .

We have the problem of two Empires that have disappeared, Russia and Turkey. . . . You do not want to divide the loot; that would be a wrong policy for the future. You must make some arrangement which will conserve the peace of the world in the future, and give some form of decent government for these countries. It seems to me the League of Nations . . . should become the titular reversionary for these Empires. If there is to be any title in the future, any supreme authority, any supreme control in the future in respect of these countries that have fallen off from Russia and Turkey, it should be the League of Nations, and they should combine the principles of autonomy and self-determination.[8]

Smuts clearly conceived of the League of Nations maintaining peace and order in eastern Europe and the Middle East. He did not envisage the same type of 'mandatory rule' over the German colonies. Though he was prepared to admit a certain amount of international control by the League of Nations over tropical Africa (but not, at this stage, South-West Africa—the idea was the same as his one of a 'Development Board'), Smuts and his colleagues regarded the African questions as basically different from the ones of Europe and the Middle East. They confidently thought that the principle of self-determination would work in Britain's favour if used with the Arabs of the

of my public life has been spent in connection with the political ambitions of France, which I have come across in Tunis, in Siam, and in almost every distant region where the French have sway. We have been brought, for reasons of national safety, into an alliance with the French, which I hope will last, but their national character is different from ours, and their political interests collide with our own in many cases. I am seriously afraid that the great Power from whom we may have most to fear in the future is France, and I almost shudder at the possibility of putting France in such a position. She is powerful in almost all parts of the world, even around India'. Eastern Committee Minutes, Secret, 2 Dec. 1918, CAB. 27/24.

[8] *Ibid.* See also Smuts's pamphlet, *The League of Nations: a Practical Suggestion* (London, 1918); and Hancock, *Smuts*, chap. XX.

former Turkish territories; but they viewed it as an unknown and dangerous formula to apply to the inhabitants of the German colonies. 'We must not allow ourselves', Balfour said, 'to be driven by that broad principle [of self-determination] into applying it pedantically where it is really inapplicable, namely, to wholly barbarous, undeveloped and unorganised black tribes, whether they be in the Pacific or Africa. Self-determination there, I do not say it has no meaning . . . , but evidently you cannot transfer formulas more or less applicable to the populations of Europe to these utterly different races'.[9] Even in the German colonies there appeared to be different 'stages of civilization' between the negroes of tropical Africa and the more primitive peoples, according to Smuts, of South-West Africa and the Pacific. Taken together—the inhabitants of the Middle East, Africa and the Pacific—there appeared to be three distinguishable classes. At the Peace Conference they became known as 'A', 'B', and 'C'. The 'C' class found its way into the mandates system only because of Wilson's unyielding insistence.

During the discussions of the Imperial War Cabinet in December, the Prime Ministers of the southern Dominions had proclaimed that under no circumstances could Wilson be permitted to interfere with the annexation of South-West Africa and the islands in the southern Pacific. Lloyd George had supported their views. 'One thing was quite certain', he is reported to have said on the 20th, 'and that was that none of Germany's colonies would be returned to her. Another thing that was certain was that those colonies which had been captured by Dominion troops must be retained by the Dominions concerned, such as the Pacific colonies south of the Equator, and German South-West Africa'.[10] Lord Milner urged that from the outset it should be made clear that South-West Africa and the Pacific islands should be treated 'as belonging to the Dominions concerned'. His ideas in this respect coincided with those of the Prime Minister of Australia.

Mr. Hughes suggested that, both as regards the Pacific Islands, which were in the immediate neighbourhood of Australia, and presumably in the case of German South-West Africa, the differen-

[9] Eastern Committee Minutes, Secret, 5 Dec. 1918, CAB. 27/24.
[10] Imperial War Cabinet Minutes, Secret, 20 Dec. 1918, CAB 23/42.

tiating of their occupation from that of the adjoining Dominion would create insuperable difficulties in respect of customs laws, coastwise trade, methods of economic development, labour laws, &c.

Australia's claim to the islands, Hughes said, was being put forward 'in the interests of Australian security' and his country would not tolerate any external interference.[11] Expressing those views time and time again at the Imperial War Cabinet meetings, Hughes emerged as the stalwart champion of the interests of the southern Dominions and strident critic of President Wilson. The League of Nations and its cumbersome apparatus of a mandates system, according to Hughes, was to Wilson 'what a toy was to a child—he would not be happy till he got it'.[12] Wilson, with childlike ignorance, in Hughes's opinion, had no grasp over the problems of the Pacific. 'He thought that President Wilson was talking of a problem which he did not really understand. New Guinea was only 80 miles from Australia'. If the British annexed the islands in the southern Pacific, Wilson apparently thought that he would have no grounds for objecting to the permanent Japanese occupation of the ones north of the Line. But Wilson, according to Hughes, had failed to produce any sensible solution to the problem. Hughes thought it preposterous that the League of Nations somehow might assume responsibility for the islands. 'President Wilson', he said, ' . . . had no practical scheme at all, and no proposals that would bear the test of experience. . . . It was intolerable . . . for President Wilson to dictate to us how the world was to be governed'.[13]

Hughes's attacks on Wilson disturbed the powerful advocates of a colonial *pax Anglo-Americana*, Borden, Smuts and Milner.

---

[11] *Ibid*. At this meeting of the Imperial War Cabinet, Hughes read into the record that in 1917 Australia 'simply accepted the inevitable' by adhering to the Anglo-Japanese understanding, which carried with it British support of Japanese claims to the German islands north of the Equator. This was a retreat from his position a few months earlier. In August 1918 he had maintained that Australia had not been consulted about the Anglo-Japanese negotiations and the following November wrote a 'Most Secret' letter to Lloyd George reminding him that Australia 'profoundly distrusts Japan'. For that letter (4 Nov. 1918) and the Foreign Office's refutation of Hughes's charge that the Australian Government had not been kept informed about the Anglo-Japanese negotiations, see F.O. 371/3236.

[12] Imperial War Cabinet Minutes, Secret, 30 Dec. 1918, CAB. 23/42.

[13] *Ibid*.

'If the policy of the British Empire meant working in co-operation with some European nation as against the United States', Borden said after one of Hughes's outbursts, 'that policy could not reckon on the approval or support of Canada'. Borden, like Wilson, did not believe that the war had been fought 'in order to add territory to the British Empire'. He was prepared to support the annexationist claims of the southern Dominions, but he thought that if the result of the war was simply a scramble for territory by the Allies, 'it would be merely a prelude to further wars'.[14] Like Smuts and Milner, he thought that the United States should be encouraged to accept 'world-wide responsibilities in respect of undeveloped territories and backward races'. All three attached supreme importance to an Anglo-American 'colonial alliance'. According to Lord Milner: 'the future peace of the world depended on a good understanding between us [Britain and the United States] and [he] regarded this policy of a mandate by the League of Nations, not as a mere cloak for annexation, but as a bond of union . . . between the United States and ourselves'.[15] Those ideas were also shared by Lloyd George, who fully saw the advantages of bringing America into the mainstream of colonial affairs.

If America were to go away from the [Peace] Conference with her share of guardianship, it would have a great effect on the world. . . . by making the offer to America we would remove any prejudice against us on the ground of "land-grabbing".[16]

The phrases 'Guardianship', 'Trusteeship', 'Mandatory Rule' which Lloyd George and other British statesmen were fond of using meant in a strict sense merely a form of international control. According to the minutes of the Imperial War Cabinet:

[14] *Ibid.*, 20 and 30 Dec. 1918.
[15] *Ibid.*, 20 Dec. 1918; David Lloyd George, *The Truth about the Peace Treaties* (2 vols., London, 1938), I, p. 122.
[16] *Ibid.;* Lloyd George, *The Truth about the Peace Treaties*, I, p. 118. That Lloyd George published this and other similar quotations of his own bears evidence that he tried to fulfill his boast of publishing his memoirs of the Peace Conference without 'suppression or distortion of any relevant fact or document'. So far as colonial problems are concerned he seems to have suppressed little. But, owing to the limited number of sources he appears to have had at his disposal when he wrote his account, Lloyd George's history of the proceedings is now of interest less because of the evidence presented than because of the insight it gives into his personality.

... As to the precise distinction between the occupation of territory in a "possessory" and in a "mandatory" capacity ... it was generally agreed that "mandatory occupation" did not involve anything in the nature of condominium or international administration, but administration by a single Power on certain lines laid down by the League of Nations. These lines would naturally include equality of treatment to all nations in respect of tariffs, concessions, and economic policy generally.[17]

By attaching that meaning to 'mandates', Lloyd George and his colleagues believed that the British could get their share of the spoils but not commit themselves to obligations any more stringent than those Britain had already incurred in tropical Africa under the Berlin and Brussels Acts of 1885 and 1890.[18] By accepting mandates along the lines of those Acts, they hoped to pay little for an object of great value: American friendship in colonial affairs.

Would the United States be willing, in Milner's words, 'to become one of the mandatories and share in the white man's burden?' Curzon doubted it; if they were willing, he hoped they would channel their energies into a place where the British had no strategic interest. Along the same lines Milner thought that Armenia might be a possibility. 'The mere fact that we did not want it ourselves was no reason for not assigning the responsibility of it to the United States'. Winston Churchill on the other hand thought that it would be dangerous to entrust even Armenia to the Americans:

... If America were introduced in the heart of European politics, in Armenia, or anywhere else in the Mediterranean region, this would be an incentive to her to make herself the greatest Naval Power.[19]

[17] Imperial War Cabinet Minutes, Secret, 20 Dec. 1918, CAB. 23/42.
[18] This was the analogy used by Lloyd George at the Peace Conference. *Papers relating to the Foreign Relations of the United States: the Paris Peace Conference, 1919* (13 vols., Washington, 1942–47), III, p. 750.
[19] Imperial War Cabinet Minutes, Secret, 20 Dec. 1918, CAB. 23/42. 'Admiral Wemyss supported this argument and said the Admiralty would regard a large American fleet in the Mediterranean with greater apprehension than anywhere else. An American occupation of Palestine, or Armenia, would inevitably lead to her building up a fleet in the Mediterranean, with bases and lines of communication'.

If the British had to give up any territory to the Americans, Churchill was 'strongly in favour of giving up German East Africa'. Lloyd George also preferred an African solution. Previously he had supported the proposal of shoving the Americans into Palestine. He now in late December explained why he preferred East Africa. If the Americans accepted a mandate for Palestine:

It would involve placing an absolutely new and crude Power in the middle of all our complicated interests in Egypt, Arabia, and Mesopotamia. Everyone with any complaint to make against British administration would rush off to the United States, who would not be able to resist the temptation to meddle. Every Bedouin would be going to the Americans, and we should be put into the humiliating position of continually giving in to the Americans on every complaint raised by them, up to a point when we could stand it no longer, and then might find ourselves involved in a serious quarrel.[20]

Compared with the withdrawal of British influence from Palestine, the transfer of German East Africa in Lloyd George's opinion was 'the least undesirable alternative'. Smuts however put forward his powerful strategic reason why Britain should become the mandatory power in East Africa:

The British Empire was the great African Power right along the eastern half of the continent, and securing East Africa would give us through communication along the whole length of the continent—a matter of the greatest importance from the point of view of both land and of air communications. . . . It was not only on the grounds of our conquests and sacrifices, but on the obvious geographical situation, that we were entitled to make a strong claim to being the mandatory in that region. Personally he would give up very much in order to attain that. . . . He would prefer to see the United States in Palestine rather than East Africa.[21]

The Imperial War Cabinet thus still did not agree on where the United States should assume mandatory responsibilities. As the Secretary of State for India summed up the result of these pre-

---

[20] *Ibid.*

[21] 'Mr. Balfour suggested that the line of argument pursued by General Smuts was perhaps playing a little fast-and-loose with the notion of mandatory occupation'. Imperial War Cabinet Minutes, Secret, 20 Dec. 1918 CAB. 23/42; Lloyd George, *The Truth about the Peace Treaties*, I, pp. 119–20.

Conference discussions: 'we seem to be drifting into the position that right from the east to the west there is only one possible solution of all our difficulties, namely, that Great Britain should accept responsibility for all these countries. For some reason, France is objectionable *here*; for other reasons, America is objectionable *there*, and the only solution is that we should be the tutelary Power'.[22]

The discussions about the German colonies on the eve of the Peace Conference amounted above all to this: how to cope with President Wilson? That problem was closely connected with the one of how to deal with the French and the Italians. By accepting mandates the British hoped to satisfy Wilson's demand for a disinterested colonial settlement and at the same time to honour their secret obligations to France and Italy. So far as Africa was concerned, that did not seem to be difficult. As Smuts said to the Imperial War Cabinet, most of the Cameroons and Togoland had already been given to the French and 'it was really only a question of boundaries'.[23] The Italians demanded fair compensation under the terms of the Treaty of London, but Balfour hoped that they could be foisted off 'with an enlargement of the frontiers of Tripoli, &c'.[24] The German colonies themselves therefore did not seem to pose any great difficulties among the Allies. But they did if they were considered in relation to other territorial questions, especially those of the Middle

[22] Eastern Committee Minutes, Secret, 9 Dec. 1918, CAB. 27/24.

[23] Long reluctantly agreed that the best the British could do was to claim the small parts of West Africa allotted to them by the agreements of 1914 and 1916. But he was remorseful that the Foreign Office had given away so much. 'Mr. Long explained to Mr. Lloyd George, with the aid of a map, the importance of Duala. He pointed out that this was the best port on the west coast of Africa, and possessed great importance as a potential base for coal and oil supplies, and a wireless station. Mr. Long said that Sir Frederick Lugard, who had a very wide knowledge of African questions, was of opinion that the portions of the Cameroons which we had from time to time been anxious to get were of little value, and he would be inclined to give the whole of the Cameroons and Togoland to France. Further, Sir Frederick contested that the argument that a certain coast district was wanted as a health resort was ludicrous, as anyone who wanted such a resort could come to England just as easily. He (Mr. Long) was, however, averse from giving up anything'. Imperial War Cabinet Minutes, Secret, 20 Dec. 1918, CAB. 23/42. In his memoirs Lloyd George remarked that Long was the only member of the Government who could be accused of 'avidity'. *The Truth about the Peace Treaties*, I, p. 116.

[24] Minutes of the Imperial War Cabinet, Secret, 23 Dec. 1918, CAB. 23/42.

East. Considering the far reaching British claims and spheres of influence extended by the war, it might appear to those who did not distinguish between the Imperial Government and those of the Dominions that 'an already bloated British Empire', as Smuts once put it, had gobbled up the colonial spoils while France and Italy had become emaciated on the battlefields of Europe. To most members of the Imperial War Cabinet that was an unfair conclusion to draw. According to Curzon:

After all, our great territorial occupation during this war was the inevitable result of our previous position as a colonising Power, in consequence of which we were already contiguous to the enemy in those regions.[25]

Whatever the French and Italians might have thought of that explanation, they clearly were jealous of British gains and their ambitions would have repercussions on questions upon which the Allies had already reached agreement, above all on the German colonies. In return for granting British demands in the Middle East, the French and the Italians might insist that the British yield more of the German territories. As Balfour and Cecil once summed up the problem:

Balfour: ... the French and the Italians. They are not in the least out for self-determination, they are out for getting whatever they can.
Cecil: They are Imperialists.
Balfour: Exactly. They are Imperialistic, and quite frankly so.[26]

Considering the complexity of the world-wide territorial problems and the necessity of cooperating with the French, Balfour hankered for a return to the Entente diplomacy before the war.

If I were to go to the French to-morrow and say, "Will you make common cause with us against everybody; we will support everything you want which does not affect our interests, and you must support everything which does not affect your interests," I have not a doubt that we should come to an agreement. We should come to it at the cost of our friendship ... with Italy, probably; but it could be done. ...
All the troubles of the Foreign Office, since I have been a member of it, have been brought about by matters raised by officials looking

[25] *Ibid.*, 20 Dec. 1918.
[26] Eastern Committee Minutes, Secret, 18 Dec. 1918, CAB. 27/24.

after the twopenny-halfpenny and very often very corrupt interests of France or Italy, or serving small, narrow, nationalist objects. They have raised endless friction with the Foreign Office, and if we could really leave the French and Italians in their own areas, without ever interfering with them, and bring about reciprocity, I believe the greatest British interests would be served. . . . Something like we did in the original *Entente* arrangement of 1904 would be a perfect godsend. . . .[27]

Balfour nevertheless rejected that line of thinking. He and the other members of the Imperial War Cabinet aimed at securing a stable world and the preservation of British power. In the final analysis they judged that the only way of achieving that was to cooperate with the colossus now assuming world power, the United States. In the realm of colonial affairs, the price of American friendship was the acceptance of the mandates system. From the British point of view it was an expedient and not an entirely satisfactory solution. Balfour summed up the main objection to it when he said:

What we want is a permanent settlement, a permanent peace in that part of the world. A mandatory Power from the nature of the case, [is] transitory; that is to say, it may be transitory. The mandatory Power holds his land upon a lease. He holds it indefinitely; but it is only a lease. It is not held in possession.[28]

The southern Dominions, at least, aimed at complete security of tenure in the German colonies under their control. Whether they would be able to achieve that seemed to depend entirely on President Wilson.

*   *   *

Wilson's precise ideas about mandatory rule became clear to the British statesmen only during the course of the Peace Conference, which convened formally in Paris on 18 January 1919. On his way to Europe Wilson had toyed with the idea of small nations administering the German colonies as 'common property' of the League of Nations.[29] After his arrival in Paris

[27] *Ibid.*, 9 and 18 Dec. 1918.
[28] Eastern Committee Minutes, Secret, 23 Dec. 1918, CAB. 27/24.
[29] Diary of G. L. Beer (typescript copy at the Library of Congress), 10 Dec. 1918. According to Paul Birdsall, *Versailles Twenty Years After* (New York, 1941), 'the proposal to entrust colonial administration to small states was a desperate device to avoid even the semblance of a division of spoils at the Peace Conference' (p. 42). See my article, 'The United States and the African Peace Settlement of 1919'.

he apparently modified his views after he had appraised more realistically the colonial aims of the Allies. He now saw the extent to which he might influence the colonial settlement. He abandoned his idea of trying to bring small nations free from the taint of imperialism into the colonial system; but he insisted that *all* conquered colonial territories be placed under the League of Nations—even South-West Africa and the Pacific islands. His ideas alarmed the representatives of the southern Dominions. Smuts wrote to Lloyd George that Wilson might be more inclined to acquiesce in British claims if the United States were offered a definite mandate:

I am profoundly impressed with the necessity of your urging the Americans to bear their share of responsibility for the future peace arrangements of Europe. The U.S. *must* become a mandatary in some territory of first class importance. . . . in return they may be willing to give us a free hand in respect of the German Colonies and Turkish possessions claimed by us, either outright or as mandataries. [30]

Hughes in his 'Biblical Welsh' style summed up the situation in the following way:

Wilson is the God in the machine to the people outside: but his stock declines daily in spite of much fulsome and persistent puffing. Between ourselves he is rather a stick when it comes down to the facts of life. He is great on great principles. As to their application he is so much like Alice in Wonderland that I suspect him of being [sic] sat in a former incarnation for that dear little lady to Lewis Carroll. . . .

I'm working up the case for the ex-German Colonies and the Pacific. Wilson's against us on this point. . . . But I hope we shall convince him. I think we shall for he is a man firm on nothing that really matters. He regards the League of Nations as the great Charter of the World that is to be and sees himself through the roseate cloud of dreams officiating as the High Priest in the Temple in which the Sarcophagus or Ark containing the body or ashes of this amazing gift to Mankind is to rest in majestic seclusion for all time. Give *him* a League of Nations and he will give *us* all the rest. Good. He shall have his toy! [31]

[30] Smuts to Lloyd George (copy), 14 Jan. 1919, Smuts Papers.
[31] Hughes to Ferguson, Personal, 17 Jan. 1919, Novar Papers.

With his 'old fashioned view of imperialism', as Lloyd George put it, Hughes had no intention of admitting Wilson's principle of mandatory control into the Pacific.

At the end of the first week of the conference, the British delegation still did not know how hard Wilson was prepared to fight for a universal application of the mandates system. Anxious to avoid the impression that the Peace Conference had met to divide the spoils, the President tried to postpone the colonial question as long as possible. Lloyd George, 'being anxious to know where President Wilson stood on the question of the German colonies and Turkey',[32] finally managed to get the topic on the agenda of the Supreme Council after he persuaded Wilson that time could be saved by settling the straightforward colonial issues before taking up the more complex and important European ones. On the 24th Lloyd George presented the British case to the delegates of the United States, France, Italy and Japan.[33] After Lloyd George briefly pointed out the harshness of German colonial rule, Wilson said that he thought 'all were agreed to oppose the restoration of the German colonies'. The main colonial anxiety of the British Government and public throughout the war—that Germany's colonies might be returned—was thus relieved quickly and without controversy. Lloyd George then considered the three possible solutions: internationalization, control by the League of Nations, and annexation. He assumed that all agreed that the first was impossible. As to the second, Great Britain would be willing, he said, to undertake various mandates under the control of the

[32] Minutes of the British Empire Delegation, Secret, 3, 23 Jan. 1919, CAB. 29/28/1.

[33] Among the many works which have dealt with the mandates negotiations at the Peace Conference, the more important are: Ray Stannard Baker, *Woodrow Wilson and World Settlement* (3 vols., New York, 1922); Robert Lansing, *The Peace Negotiations: A Personal Narrative* (Boston and New York, 1921); David Hunter Miller, 'The Origin of the Mandates System', *Foreign Affairs*, VI (1928); *The Intimate Papers of Colonel House*, ed. Charles Seymour (4 vols., New York and Boston, 1928); Quincy Wright, *Mandates under the League of Nations* (Chicago, 1930); Seth P. Tillman, *Anglo-American Relations at the Paris Peace Conference of 1919* (Princeton, 1961); and the works cited in footnotes of this chapter. The best general work on the subject is H. Duncan Hall, *Mandates, Dependencies and Trusteeship* (Washington, 1948). For a discussion of these and other works, see my essay in *The Historiography of the British Empire-Commonwealth*, ed. Robin W. Winks (Durham, 1966).

League of Nations. After a brief consideration of how the third possibility, annexation, might apply to some of the colonies, he introduced Hughes, Massey and Smuts to present the cases for the southern Dominions. Hughes argued, among other things, that the islands claimed by his Government 'were as necessary to Australia as water to a city'; Smuts stated that South-West Africa was a mere desert best absorbed into South Africa; and Massey pleaded that Samoa was a place of great strategic importance in the Pacific where the New Zealanders were doing their best to bring civilization. All three cases rested on the argument that the territories in question were geographically part of the neighbouring Dominion and would be a strategic menace unless annexed. To put it in a different way, as Smuts did privately in regard to South-West Africa, the arguments were 'like the poor sinning girl's plea that her baby was only a very little one!'[34] Lloyd George said a few days later that the British Empire had made out 'a very strong case'.[35]

After hearing the presentation of Japanese claims to take over German rights in Shantung and to annex the islands north of the Equator, Wilson on 27 January expanded fully for the first time his ideas about mandatory control.

This he assumed to be the principle: it was not intended to exploit any people; it was not intended to exercise arbitrary sovereignty over any people.

The purpose was to serve the people in undeveloped parts, to safeguard them against abuses such as had occurred under German administration and such as might be found under other administrations. Further, where people and territories were undeveloped, to assure their development so that, when the time came, their own interests, as they saw them, might qualify them to express a wish as to their ultimate relations—perhaps lead them to desire their union with the mandatory power.[36]

He used South-West Africa and New Guinea as examples, thus making it abundantly clear that he rejected the annexationist claims of the southern Dominions. 'The fundamental idea', he

[34] Smuts to M. C. Gillet, 25 Jan. 1919, Smuts Papers, quoted in *Selections from the Smuts Papers*, IV, pp. 55–56.

[35] Minutes of the British Empire Delegation, Secret, 4, 27 Jan. 1919, CAB. 29/28/1.

[36] *Foreign Relations, Paris Peace Conference*, III, pp. 740–41; CAB. 28/6.

said, 'would be that the world was acting as trustee through a mandatory, and would be in charge of the whole administration until the day when the true wishes of the inhabitants could be ascertained'. He implied that the natives of South-West Africa 'would eventually come into the Union of their own free will'; but—indicative of the antagonism felt by Wilson towards Hughes—he said that his mind was 'absolutely open' to a possible mandatory power in New Guinea. Australia might become the guardian there because of proximity, but the question, Wilson said, was 'in the lap of the Gods'.[37] His speech drew rejoinders from the Prime Ministers of South Africa and Australia. Botha said that he was an enthusiast for the League of Nations, but that for the sake of peace South-West Africa would have to be incorporated into the Union. Hughes attacked the mandatory principle itself.[38] 'Was the mandatory principle *per se* desirable?', he asked.

There was nothing to be gained by the mandatory system that could not be got by direct Government, except that the World was said to dread annexations. But he was positive that no one dreaded the annexation of New Guinea by Australia. The world only dreaded annexation for Imperialistic purposes or for the purpose of exploiting other peoples. But Australia was a democracy and responsible for its actions to its people. He would readily admit that the mandatory system would be applicable to other parts; but it could never apply to New Guinea.[39]

That evening the British Empire Delegation considered Wilson's attitude. Smuts began the tactical retreat he had outlined the previous November. He and Lord Robert Cecil had decided that the mandatory principle should be divided into three classes:

(1) German Colonies with a British Dominion next door. In these cases there should be annexation. For many reasons it was impossible to make a Dominion into a mandatory.
(2) German Colonies in Central Africa. These to be distinguished from the first class by the circumstances that the world, as a whole,

[37] *Ibid.*, pp. 741–43.
[38] The arguments used by Hughes were remarkably similar to those used by Wilson's own Secretary of State, Robert Lansing. See Lansing's book, *The Peace Negotiations*, chap. XIII.
[39] *Foreign Relations, Paris Peace Conference*, III, pp. 746–47.

was interested in them. They were cases for a mandatory, but on the basis that the mandatory should be a Power with sovereign rights subject, however, to restrictions in relation to arms, liquor, &c., and the open door. Great Britain and France should be the mandatories in Central Africa, and should bear any expense involved.

(3) Other cases where the people of the territories in question could speak for themselves, but where they required assistance in government and in the development of the country, e.g., Syria and Mesopotamia. At this point the subject became part of the subject of the League of Nations.[40]

Despite the implied division of the three classes of territories (which shortly were to become, in inverse order, the 'A', 'B' and 'C' mandates) the British Empire Delegation still refused to admit that South-West Africa and the Pacific islands should fall under the influence of the League of Nations.[41]

The next morning, the 28th, Lloyd George stated before the Supreme Council that the Dominions had a 'special case' and that he hoped President Wilson would look into it again. Massey then gave a rambling defence of New Zealand's claims to Samoa and asked Wilson what George Washington would have done if the territories of North America had been placed as mandates under a league of nations after the war of independence. Wilson sharply corrected Massey's historical interpretations. That afternoon the French Colonial Minister joined the Prime Ministers of the southern Dominions by proclaiming himself in favour of 'annexation, pure and simple'. It was the only way, in his opinion, that colonial governments worthy of the name could achieve their objectives.[42] Wilson exploded. The discussions so far, he said, had been 'a negation in detail— one case at a time—of the whole principle of mandatories'. Warning that 'it looked as if their roads diverged', he thought it best to discontinue the discussions in order to avoid disagreement. After some soothing remarks by Balfour and Lloyd George, Wilson pointedly remarked that Australia claimed

[40] Minutes of the British Empire Delegation, Secret, 4, 27 Jan. 1919, CAB. 29/28/1.
[41] 'Mr. Lloyd George said that the British position had been quite clear up to the present. It had been this—there should be no application of the mandatory principle in the case of the Colonies claimed by Australia, South Africa and New Zealand'. *Ibid.*
[42] *Foreign Relations, Paris Peace Conference*, III, pp. 749–63.

sovereignty over New Guinea, the Union of South Africa over South-West Africa, Japan over the leased territory in Shantung and the Pacific islands, and that France demanded a sort of 'modified' sovereignty over the West African territories. He rejoiced in the only exception: the colonies taken by troops under direct control by the government in London. The rest had rejected the idea of trusteeship. He asked, how would that look to the rest of the world?

The world would say that the Great Powers first portioned out the helpless parts of the world, and then formed a League of Nations. The crude fact would be that each of these parts of the world had been assigned to one of the Great Powers.[43]

The Italian Prime Minister, alarmed at Wilson's omission of Italy as a power claiming spoils, said he favoured the trustee-ship idea and that Italy would be willing to accept colonial responsibilities under any equitable terms. Clemenceau, who thought France could achieve her colonial objectives regardless of Wilson's scheme, repudiated his Colonial Minister and stated that he 'would be guided by the judgment of his colleagues'.[44] The southern Dominions held out. Lloyd George said to the British Empire Delegation the next morning that he 'feared a deadlock, and that the President would leave this country before an agreement had been reached'.[45] The colonial issue at this stage thus threatened to disrupt the proceedings of the Peace Conference.

Using all of his political ingenuity, Lloyd George by cajoling and bullying the Prime Ministers of Australia and New Zealand got them to accept a compromise proposal by which South-West Africa and the Pacific islands also would become mandates, but ones administered as 'integral portions' of the mandatory powers.[46] If Hughes thought Great Britain was going to quarrel with the United States about a few islands,

---

[43] Ibid., pp. 765–66   [44] Ibid., pp. 767–71.
[45] Minutes of the British Empire Delegation, Secret, 6, 29 Jan. 1919, CAB. 29/28/1.
[46] During the British Empire Delegation meeting on the afternoon of the 28th, 'It was agreed that Mr. Hughes, General Botha, and Mr. Massey should draft a resolution to express the view of the Delegation with respect to the Mandatory System'. Apparently J. G. Latham of the Australian delegation penned the actual draft that evening under the supervision of Smuts and Hankey.

Lloyd George said, the Australian Prime Minister was very much mistaken. Undaunted, Hughes stood up to Lloyd George and fought 'like a weasel—which he somewhat resembles—for annexation in the Pacific'.[47] At one meeting of the British Empire Delegation he lashed out at the British Prime Minister with 'some burning words about men, who forgetful of their high office, the great traditions of the British people and their heroic valour and immense sacrifices in the war, prostrated themselves in meek subservience before the representative of America. . . '.[48] In his calmer moments Hughes asked whether Wilson had any definite ideas about the precise application of 'mandatory control'. Smuts thought not—'he was satisfied that President Wilson had no tangible idea on the subject'. In return for nominal acceptance of the trusteeship principle, Wilson might be willing to give the Australasians all but complete control over the southern Pacific islands. Cecil assured Hughes that under the mandates system Australia would have 'absolute security' and that the Australian Government only would have to 'report annually' to the League of Nations. Hughes brushed aside that requirement as 'an appeal from the men who knew to those who did not know'.[49] That obligation did not seem to bother him. What Hughes and Massey aimed at above all was complete control over immigration and trade—so that the 'White Australia' policy could be enforced. Assured that the 'C' class of mandate would close the 'open door' (which remained 'open' in the 'B' and 'A' classes) and that the Japanese would be prevented from 'infiltrating' into

[47] Green to Lambert, 29 Jan. 1919, C.O. 537/1020.

[48] 'And then having exhausted my stock of vituperative language in English, I fell back upon Welsh—the ideal language for giving full expression to the emotions and passions. And believe me, as our friends in America would put it, I said "a mouthful". My words poured out in a foaming cataract: they were highly personal, the kind of words even the most conventional of men would on occasion dearly love to use, but for what the prim and proper people all round them would think. To the members of the Cabinet staring at me open mouthed, they were words full of sound and fury without any definite meaning, but they hit Lloyd George between wind and water. He knew what they meant all right; but he had not heard anything like them since he was a boy!' W. M. Hughes, *Policies and Potentates* (Sydney, 1950). Hughes evidently based that passage on a post-Second World War memorandum entitled 'Mandate and Racial Equality Clause' in the Hughes Papers.

[49] Minutes of the British Empire Delegation, Secret, 5, 28 Jan. 1919, CAB. 29/28/1.

the islands, Hughes and Massey finally acquiesced. They were content, Hughes wrote later, knowing that the 'C' mandates 'gave the Mandatory power the same authority over the mandated territory as it had over its own country, differing from full sovereign control as a nine hundred and ninety years' lease differs from a fee simple'.[50]

On the morning of the 30th Lloyd George circulated to the Supreme Council the draft proposal of the 'A', 'B' and 'C' mandates. He carefully stated that it did not reflect the 'real views' of the Dominions and that it had been agreed upon in a spirit of compromise. Wilson however was not in a conciliatory mood that morning. He was highly annoyed at an article planted by Hughes in the Paris edition of the *Daily Mail* which described the American President as an impractical idealist. Though Wilson granted that Lloyd George's proposal brought them closer to agreement, he said there could be no final decision at the moment. He never accepted an ideal, he said, 'until he could see its practical application'. Pointing his remarks towards Hughes, Wilson stated that no one could say definitely that Australia would become the mandatory power in New Guinea. 'In every instance the mandate should fit the case as the glove fits the hand'. Lloyd George exclaimed that the President's remarks filled him with despair. Wilson replied that he accepted the British proposal as a 'provisional arrangement' and that he had said 'nothing which need justify discouragement'. That statement filled Hughes with rage. What was he to tell the people of Australia, he asked. Merely that the mandates system would 'fit like a glove to the hand'? He wanted precise answers—and a definite and immediate settlement.[51] In the afternoon session Massey also attacked what he considered to be the President's tactics of delay and equivocation. Wilson gathered that Hughes and Massey refused to subscribe to the trusteeship principle and were renewing their annexationist claims. He asked whether Australia and New Zealand had presented 'an ultimatum to the whole civilized world'. Hughes replied, 'That's about the size of it, President Wilson'.[52]

[50] Memorandum by Hughes, 'Mandate and Racial Equality Clause', no date but post-Second World War, Hughes Papers.
[51] *Foreign Relations, Paris Peace Conference*, III, pp. 785-94.
[52] The official minutes record Hughes as saying 'President Wilson had

At that emotionally charged stage of the discussion Botha intervened. As the Prime Minister of the southern Dominion whose security was affected as much by South-West Africa as was that of Australia and New Zealand by the islands, his words carried weight. He described the 'very serious discussion, worry and trouble' which he, Hughes and Massey had had in reaching agreement on the 'C' mandate proposal and how it was necessary to 'give way on the smaller things' in order to get to the higher ideal. 'Personally he felt very strongly about the question of German South-West Africa'. But he was willing to have South-West Africa placed under mandatory control as a step towards the realization of the ideal of a League of Nations.[53] After Botha's speech no one dissented from the proposal to establish 'A', 'B' and 'C' mandates.

At the same meeting on the 30th, the French, Italian and Belgian delegates raised important points about the future administration and distribution of the mandates. Pichon, the French Minister for Foreign Affairs, said that France could not entirely support part of Article 7 of the proposal, which read that the mandatory power was responsible 'for the prevention of the military training of the natives for other than police purposes'. He contended that the French military position during the war would have been critical without the assistance of colonial troops. Clemenceau demanded that France should have 'the right of raising troops in case of general war'. The minutes of the Supreme Council read:

Mr. Lloyd George said that so long as M. Clemenceau did not train big nigger armies for the purposes of aggression, that was all the clause was intended to guard against.

M. Clemenceau said that he did not want to do that. He therefore understood that Mr. Lloyd George's interpretation was adopted.

President Wilson said that Mr. Lloyd George's interpretation was consistent with the phraseology.[54]

put it fairly well', but Hughes's biographer, L. F. Fitzhardinge, believes that the above version is authentic. He discusses Hughes's role in the peace negotiations in an unpublished paper, 'W. M. Hughes and the Treaty of Versailles, 1919'.
[53] *Foreign Relations, Paris Peace Conference*, III, pp. 797–802.
[54] *Ibid.*, pp. 804–05.

Perhaps unintentionally, Wilson thus compromised his principle of demilitarization.[55] In final form the clause bound the French not to establish military or naval bases in their mandated territories; but a special clause (not included in the other mandate contracts) authorized them to raise troops in the case of war. Clemenceau said he was 'quite satisfied' with the outcome of the discussion. The Italian Prime Minister, Orlando, had less reason to be pleased. So far there had been no indication that Italy would be invited to become one of the mandatory powers. He put the question indirectly. How would the mandates be conferred? Clemenceau summed up the Italian point more bluntly: 'His [Orlando's] proposal was that as France, England and her Dominions had had their share, Italy wanted to have her own share'. But Wilson for the moment wanted to avoid the question of apportioning the mandates. He gave the following reason:

Many of these mandates would constitute a burden—by no means a privilege—and a very serious burden, but while he should not [sic] be disinclined to see the United States get any advantage out of this war, he should be equally disinclined to see her shirk any burden or duty. But he could think of nothing the people of the United States would be less inclined to accept than military responsibility in Asia. If the United States of America, therefore, was to be asked to share a burden of mandates, the request would have to be postponed until he could explain the whole matter to them, and try to bring them to the point of view which he desired them to assume.[56]

Wilson's colonial adviser interpreted that statement to mean that the President had made the momentous decision that the United States should accept mandates.[57] In any case Wilson

[55] Wilson's colonial adviser, G. L. Beer, thought that 'Clemenceau understood the agreement in a diametrically opposite sense from that of Wilson and Lloyd George' and tried to block the French 'black army' scheme during the discussions of the Mandates Commission. The agreement of 30 Jan. was explicit, however, and the French right 'to raise troops in case of general war' was incorporated eventually in the mandates for Togoland and the Cameroons. On this point see especially Miller, 'The Origin of the Mandates System', and Birdsall, *Versailles Twenty Years After*, chap. III.

[56] *Foreign Relations, Paris Peace Conference*, III, pp. 805–07.

[57] 'Very exciting sessions. Wilson's announcement that he was prepared to have U.S.A. assume mandates aroused no excitement and its significance was not noticed'. Beer's Diary, 30 Jan. 1919.

was determined to postpone the assignment of the mandates—which he feared would appear in the eyes of the public as a division of the spoils—as long as possible. He was startled to learn that even the Belgians were clamouring for an immediate African settlement. At the close of the meeting on the 30th, Clemenceau announced that the Belgian delegates wished to speak about the 'Congo'. Lloyd George, who knew that German East Africa would be the subject of their discourse, 'said that the Congo was not a German conquest' and that the Belgian request seemed irrelevant. Clemenceau however insisted that it would be 'a little harsh' not to hear them. The Belgians were ushered in. The colonial adviser to the Belgian Foreign Ministry gave a summary of events in central Africa during the war and put forward Belgian claims to the northwestern part of German East Africa. After the Belgians had departed Lloyd George complained that they had raised a question that had not yet been discussed: who would be the mandatory power in German East Africa? Wilson added sarcastically that the real question was 'how to divide up East Africa'.[58] He clearly saw that he was in the middle of a colonial scramble. Nevertheless he had won the day by the acceptance of the trusteeship principle: the Turkish territories and all of the German colonies would be placed under the control of the League of Nations.

The British press generally gave the mandates system a hostile reception. Even newspapers and periodicals favourable to Wilson's scheme such as *The Times*, the *Daily Chronicle*, the *Manchester Guardian* and the *New Statesman*, doubted whether South-West Africa and the Pacific islands should have been placed under international control. According to the *Observer*, the southern Dominions should 'at the very least be the perpetual mandatories over countries in which their interest so overwhelmingly outweighs the rest of the world's'.[59] On the political left such writers as John A. Hobson denounced the mandates system as 'a thin veil for the annexation of enemy countries and the division of the spoil'.[60] On the right the

[58] *Foreign Relations, Paris Peace Conference*, III, pp. 808–12.
[59] 2 Feb. 1919.
[60] In a letter to the editor of *Common Sense*, 5 Mar. 1919. Along these lines see also especially the comments of the *Herald*, 8 Feb. 1919: 'What a mandatory is or is supposed to do remains mysterious. It may be that the whole "mandatory" business is intended as mere dust in the eyes of

conservative newspapers such as the *Globe* attacked the business of 'GIVING AWAY THE EMPIRE. . . . International control sooner or later, means German control. For what purpose, then, will the war have been fought?'[61] The *Pall Mall Gazette* pointed out: 'a mandate which the League of Nations can give, it can also take away . . . the mandatory system may easily betray us into a hopeless tangle of conflicting rights and obligations'.[62] The military correspondent of the *Morning Post* pinned the blame on Smuts for having given publicity to the idea in his pamphlet, *The League of Nations: a Practical Suggestion.*

General Smuts is hoist by his own petard. In his pamphlet he applied this method of disposal to the territories of Russia, Austria, and Turkey, but excluded its operation from the captured German Colonies. President Wilson, encouraged by the pamphlet, evidently found no distinction between one set of captured territories and another, and applied to them all the Smutsian rule, to the amazement and disgust of our Dominions.[63]

According to a leading article in the *Morning Post*, the British delegates in Paris, by acquiescing in the mandates proposal, were 'sowing the seeds of such bitter discontent in the Dominions as might disunite and disrupt the British Empire'.[64]

The South African press echoed those sentiments. Although a few newspapers gave a lukewarm greeting to the mandates system as a step towards the realization of international idealism, South African commentary on the whole was extremely critical. *De Burger*, the principal Afrikaner organ, dismissed the mandates system as a hypocritical invention of British imperialism. The English-speaking press held that South-West Africa should have been simply annexed. The *Cape Times* made its opinion clear in the title of one of its leading articles, 'The Mandatory Muddle'.[65] Throughout South African opinion ran the consoling theme that international control would make little difference. According to the *East London Daily Dispatch*:

Labour—a screen behind which the German colonies are to be annexed by the Allied Governments and exploited by Allied capitalists. It must be the duty of Labour to prevent this, and to see to it that the "mandate" is a reality, the "trustee-ship" a fact'.

[61] 30 Jan. 1919.
[62] 30 Jan. 1919.   [63] 31 Jan. 1919.
[64] 30 Jan. 1919.   [65] 4 Feb. 1919.

Now international control is no new thing. ... In practice it [the mandates system] will probably mean that Britain or her Dominions will take over the management of most of Germany's late colonies and administer them in accordance with the well-established British colonial policy.

Nominally the mandatory Power will be the trustee of the League of Nations, but actually she will have a free hand in the administration of the new territories, so long as her system of government is not in conflict with the principles for which the League stands.[66]

The periodical *South Africa* stated the point at the back of everyone's mind more sharply:

If South-West Africa is not annexed to the Union, we do not know what annexation is. It will remain British pink on our maps. ...

What is a mandate? What is to be the final elucidation of the mandatory theory? We know, and all South Africans know, what it must not mean. It must not mean that the natives of South-West Africa are to have any ground for supposing that if they are dissatisfied at any time with the Union Government some mysterious League across the seas will take up their imaginary grievances. The mandatory theory will have to be very carefully applied to South-West Africa, or it may easily contain the germs of future trouble.[67]

The *Grahamstown Journal* also feared that the mandatory powers 'may find themselves in an impossible position between the inhabitants on the one side and the League on the other'.[68] Possible international interference lay at the heart of South African reservations about mandatory control.

In Australia and New Zealand the press debated why Wilson had so vehemently resisted Australasian attempts to annex the Pacific territories. Did 'the President with his head in the clouds' suspect Australia of harbouring territorial ambitions in that vast ocean that somehow might endanger American security? Or did Mr. 'Pecksniff' merely believe that 'Imperialism' had to be ended in the Pacific as in other places in order to secure the peace of the world? A few petulant writers of leading articles considered questions along those lines, but the main stream of opinion held that Wilson was preoccupied by another consideration:

The Dominion delegates believe President Wilson's firm stand was due to a fear that the Japanese occupation of the Pacific Islands

[66] 3 Feb. 1919.   [67] 8 Feb. 1919.   [68] 6 Feb. 1919.

would cause a great outcry in America. . . . [His] predilection for the internationalization of the German colonies is based rather upon Japan's progress across the Pacific than from a desire to thwart the British acquisition of the islands. [69]

President Wilson prefers internationalisation to Japanese expansion in the Pacific. . . .[70]

. . . Behind Mr. Wilson's vaguely philanthropic sentiments there stands the definite political purpose of safeguarding American interests in the Pacific against possible aggression on the part of Japan.[71]

The argument developed by the antipodean press ran as follows. By placing the former German colonies in the Pacific under international control, Wilson could prevent the Japanese from fortifying those islands and from building naval bases there. He could also prevent domestic criticism that he had handed Japan strategically important territories. And through the device of the annual reports of the League of Nations, the United States would have a means of intelligence about Japanese activities that otherwise might not be available. In short, through mandatory control exerted by the League of Nations, Wilson hoped to check Japanese militarism. That interpretation commanded substantial support in Australia and New Zealand. In the words of the *Sydney Morning Herald*: 'if the islands are to be under the general protection of the League of Nations they will not be fortified, and Australia will thus be secure from a surprise attack'.[72] According to the Brisbane *Telegraph*, 'an overwhelming majority of Australians is in favour of an international guardianship of the world's security'.[73] On the other hand Hughes's point of view was sharply defended also. According to the Melbourne *Argus*, 'Mr. Hughes, Mr. Massey, and General Botha had . . . every right to strive as they did for full annexation'.[74] As Hughes himself put it, each island was 'a stepping-stone, strategically connected'. A hostile power occupying New Guinea could control Australia; therefore the answer was annexation. But it did not follow, as several organs of the Australasian press pointed out, that it was the only answer. Both Wilson and Hughes aimed at the same thing: security in the Pacific. From the Australian point of view, the Wilsonian solution in many ways made more sense than the

[69] Melbourne *Age*, 1 Feb. 1919.   [70] *Grey River Argus*, 3 Feb. 1919.
[71] *Auckland Star*, 3 Feb. 1919.   [72] *Sydney Morning Herald*, 29 Jan. 1919.
[73] Brisbane *Telegraph*, 3 Feb. 1919.   [74] Melbourne *Argus*, 3 Feb. 1919.

annexationist one. By outright annexation of the former German territories, Australia could quite possibly incur the great expense of countering Japanese activities by having to build military and naval bases near the Equator which would be vulnerable in defensive operations and of questionable value in offensive manoeuvers. On the other hand, if a demilitarized buffer zone under international control—and backed by American power—could be created north of Australia, the Japanese threat obviously would be minimized. Why then did Hughes and a large part of Australasian opinion not buy Wilson's logic? So far as Hughes is concerned, the answer in part lies in the cautious nature of his mentality. Viewing the mandates system as a 'leap in the dark', he safeguarded himself from possible criticism in the future by making it quite clear that he became a party to the scheme only under duress. But another and much more important sort of logic also motivated him. As Wilson himself once pointed out in the secret sessions of the Peace Conference, Hughes had 'a fundamental lack of faith in the League'.[75] On the whole Australasian opinion suspected along with Hughes that the mandates system might interfere with the white Australia policy. The press shared his scepticism of the League's ability to prevent fortification of the islands.[76] On the basis of the evidence available to the public at the time, it seemed to most Australians and New Zealanders that Hughes had zealously defended his country's interests. 'Who to-day will venture to say that he was wrong?'[77]

*   *   *

[75] *Foreign Relations, Paris Peace Conference*, III, p. 742.

[76] The above analysis is based on a study of the following Australasian newspapers: *Advertiser* (Adelaide), *Age* (Melbourne), *Argus* (Melbourne), *Auckland Star*, *Australian Worker*, *Brisbane Courier*, *Bulletin* (Sydney), *Daily News*, *Daily Telegraph* (Sydney), *Dominion* (Wellington), *Evening Post* (Wellington), *Evening Star* (Dunedin), *Grey River Argus*, *Lyttelton Times*, *Marlborough Express* (Blenheim), *New Zealand Herald*, *New Zealand Observer*, *New Zealand Times*, *Otago Daily Times*, *Press* (Christchurch), *Poverty Bay Herald*, *Register* (Adelaide), *Southland Times*, *Sun* (Christchurch), *Sydney Morning Herald*, *Telegraph* (Brisbane), *Timaru Herald*.

[77] Adelaide *Advertiser*, 6 Feb. 1919. The question might still be asked. Had the United States joined the League, and had the League actually proved effective in preventing the Japanese from fortifying the islands, history would have taken a different course. What of history as it actually happened? In the opinion of the biographer of that fiery Australian statesman, 'history surely supports Hughes'. Fitzhardinge, 'W. M. Hughes and the Treaty of Versailles'.

Although the Peace Conference decided in late January to establish the mandates system, the mandatory powers were not appointed until early May. In the meantime the British Empire Delegation on 28 February charged the Colonial Secretary, Lord Milner—who until then had not participated in the colonial negotiations[78]—with the responsibility of clarifying the nature of mandatory rule. The task was not easy, he wrote in his report of 8 March, 'for we are opening a new chapter in International Law'. He did not concern himself with the question of sovereignty.

> I leave it to lawyers to say where the "sovereignty" will in any case reside. As it seems to me, there will in all mandated territories be in a sense a divided "sovereignty". From the practical point of view that does not appear to me to present any great difficulty. What is essential is to get rid of the existing sovereignties.[79]

Milner did not think that the drafting of the 'C' mandates would create difficulties. The 'simple and straight-forward' mandates of South-West Africa and the Pacific islands, according to him, would differ in little other than name from normal colonial possessions. The obligations incurred by the mandatory power in those cases would be 'very few and simple'. Apart from obligations to combat the slave trade and the arms traffic, and to refrain from erecting fortifications, 'this class of mandate contains no restrictions upon the legislative and administrative authority of the mandatory Power'. He continued:

> ... The country handed over to it becomes an integral part of the territory of that Power. It follows, that the commercial and fiscal system prevailing in the existing territory of the mandatory Power may be applied to the mandated territory without reservation or restriction.[80]

The 'B' mandates of tropical Africa (designed for German East Africa, Togoland and the Cameroons) were more complicated than the 'C' mandates. In Milner's opinion there were two important differences between the two classes:

---

[78] Lloyd George was extremely annoyed that Milner had not pre-arranged the various colonial settlements and curtly summoned him to Paris. See the letter in Beaverbrook, *Men and Power* (New York, 1956), pp. 330–31.

[79] Memorandum by Milner, 'Mandates', Secret, W.C.P.-211, 8 Mar. 1919, CAB. 29/9/1.

[80] *Ibid.*

(1) Under mandates of the "C" Class the laws of the mandatory Power are *ipso facto* applicable to the mandated territory, whereas in mandates of the "B" Class the mandatory Power is only made "responsible for the administration" of the mandated territory. This no doubt implies that the mandatory Power may make laws for the territory. . . . But this will have to be special legislation, and must in practice differ materially from the laws in force in the country exercising the mandates.

(2) In Class "B" mandates the mandatory Power is under very much more extensive obligations than in mandates of Class "C", especially with regard to fiscal and commercial matters. . . . It thus appears that under mandates of the "B" class, the position of a mandated territory very much resembles, if it is not absolutely identical with, that of certain existing British Protectorates such as Nigeria and East Africa, in which equality of trade conditions has already been established under existing treaties.[81]

If the 'B' mandates were more complex than those of the 'C' group, there was also, in Milner's words, a 'broad distinction in character' between these two classes on the one hand and the 'A' class on the other. The 'B' and 'C' mandates of Africa and the Pacific for all practical purposes could be regarded as colonial possessions. They were trammelled only by certain international obligations such as those to combat the slave trade, to submit reports to the League of Nations, and, in the case of the 'B' mandates, to ensure equality of commercial opportunity. Once the principle of the mandates system had been accepted by the Peace Conference in regard to the 'B' and 'C' territories, the delegates had little difficulty in drafting the terms of the mandatory obligations. This was entirely untrue of the 'A' mandates of the Middle East, which were, in Milner's words, 'by far the most difficult and complicated'. The solution to the problem of the drafting of the 'A' mandates eluded the ingenuity even of Milner, and the Middle Eastern settlement was not finally concluded until long after the Conference had adjourned.

The territorial settlements concerning the German colonies were comparatively simple, even though there were more European powers involved than in the Middle East. In the Turkish territories the only countries directly concerned were,

[81] *Ibid.*

in Milner's opinion, 'the Great European Powers' of Britain and France (he notably omitted Italy and Russia). In the Pacific and Africa the territorial controversies ensnared not only those two powers but also Australia, New Zealand, South Africa, Belgium, Portugal and Japan. The outstanding territorial question in the Far East was the Japanese claim to the German lease in Shantung and the islands north of the Equator. Though a cause of friction in Anglo-American relations, the British were bound to support Japan under the terms of the agreement of 1917. In Africa the British were obligated to honour their engagements with the French, who claimed part of Togoland and most of the Cameroons. They had no commitment to the Belgians, who demanded the northwest part of German East Africa. They also had to cope with the Italians and the Portuguese, who, though neither had conquered any territory in Africa, nevertheless demanded a share of the spoils. The Italians justified their claims on the basis of the Treaty of London; the Portuguese had no treaty engagement but could see no reason why the Portuguese Empire should not grow along with those of the other powers at Germany's expense. The Japanese, French and Belgians held far stronger positions than the Italians and Portuguese: Japanese, French and Belgian troops were in actual occupation of German colonial territory.

The British could do nothing but support Japanese claims in Shantung and the islands, despite their suspicions of Japanese ambitions. In the critical negotiations that brought the United States and Japan dangerously close to loggerheads, Lloyd George lived up to his nickname 'the goat', in another sense, by agilely jumping from one solution to another in search of a compromise which would honour British commitments to the Japanese and at the same time indicate to the Americans that his sympathy in fact lay with China. He succeeded only partially. As George Louis Beer wrote in his diary, 'the British . . . are blamed for this failure of our [American] policy in Shantung'.[82] Instead of securing the immediate restoration of Shantung to China, Wilson in late April, at the same time he was embroiled in the Fiume controversy, had to accept the Japanese promise to hand over the peninsula in full sovereignty to China,

---

[82] Beer's Diary, 30 Apr. 1919.

with Japan retaining certain economic privileges.[83] Lloyd George reported to the British Empire Delegation:

The Shantung settlement had caused much trouble. On the whole, it seemed fair to China, and while it might have been better, yet we were bound by our Treaty with Japan. The Chinese were dissatisfied, but he had pointed out to them that, but for the victory achieved by the Western Powers, Germany would have remained in Shantung and would undoubtedly have put China in a worse case even than before.[84]

The Japanese claims in Shantung make an interesting contrast to the ones of France in Morocco and of Britain in Egypt. As the representative of a power keenly interested in the affairs of the Pacific, Wilson did all he could to prevent Japanese expansion in Asia; but he did not protest against the tightening of British and French control over Africa. Drafted at the same time as the Shantung clauses of the treaty, two other sections settled the affairs of North Africa in the pattern of the Entente agreement of 1904: Britain received recognition of the protectorate declared over Egypt in 1914; France strengthened her hold over Morocco, and in addition regained in full sovereignty the two slices of the Cameroons ceded to Germany by the 1911 Moroccan agreement.[85] Egypt and Morocco thus provide another example of how the Peace Conference not only founded the mandates system but also consolidated the European empires. Wilson was perhaps powerless to prevent this, even if he had been so inclined. He intervened in European colonial affairs only in two ways: generally, by insisting on the mandates system; specifically, by attempting to check Japanese expansion in the Far East. In the African settlements he did not interfere.

The Anglo-French discussions about West Africa began in early March. Like the other African territorial questions, the problem was dealt with, in Milner's phrase,—'out of court'— not as part of the formal Conference. On 7 March Milner met with Simon, the French Colonial Minister, to discuss the

[83] For the negotiations leading to this settlement, see Fifield, *Woodrow Wilson and the Far East*, chap. V.
[84] British Empire Delegation Minutes, Secret, 30, 5 May 1919, CAB. 29/28/1.
[85] These points are discussed in my article, 'The United States and the African Peace Settlement'.

Cameroons and Togoland. According to the report of the meeting, 'M. Simon stated that his Government would be found very accommodating in the Cameroons, but could not adopt the same policy in Togoland'.[86] In the Cameroons the French willingness to accommodate the British amounted to making boundary adjustments—which were necessary, according to Milner, because (writing in reference to Togoland and German East Africa as well as the Cameroons), 'the boundaries between the different spheres of occupation are haphazard and, as a permanent arrangement, would be quite intolerable. They cut across tribal and administrative divisions, take no account of economic conditions, and are in every way objectionable. . . '. Apart from several minor adjustments designed to make this partition less artificial, the final settlement between Britain and France in the Cameroons was substantially the same as the provisional one of 1916. The Togoland negotiations were more acrimonious. 'As to Togoland, M. Simon said that, to be quite frank, France wanted the whole of it'. The French justified that claim on grounds that Dahomey had only a small seaboard 'and urgently required more'. Simon believed that Togoland was 'an entirely artificial creation'—a situation best rectified in his opinion by French annexation. Milner did not respond favourably to that suggestion: 'Lord Milner observed that he had the impression that in return for extreme accommodation on our part in the Cameroons, the French were shewing great exigence in Togoland'. Milner and Simon finally agreed that the best solution would be simply to partition Togoland between Britain and France, but to improve, as in the Cameroons, the 'very hastily fixed' provisional boundary of 1914. France received the larger part (sixty per cent of the territory, containing approximately four times the population of the British sector), which included the only good port in the colony, Lomé, and the railways running to it. Summarizing these negotiations, Milner wrote:

[86] Memorandum by C. Strachey, 'Cameroons and Togoland', 7 Mar. 1919, Milner Papers. Milner conducted these African negotiations at the Peace Conference without reference to the Colonial Office and the more important memoranda are to be found in the Milner Papers and not in the Colonial Office files. For an example of Colonial Office complaints about not knowing 'what the present position is', see C.O. to Strachey, 16 June 1919, C.O. 649/17.

While . . . the settlement is generous to France, and while we can well afford to take credit for it in any other negotiations with the French about territorial adjustments—in Syria for instance—the position from the British colonial point of view is not a bad one. We shall not, indeed, have added much to our possessions in West Africa, either in the Cameroons or in Togo. But the additional territory we have gained, though not large in extent, has a certain value in giving us better boundaries and bringing completely within our borders native Tribes which have hitherto been partly within British territory and partly outside it.[87]

The repartition of West Africa at least served the purpose of improving colonial boundaries.

Neither the Cameroons nor Togoland lay contiguous to a British Dominion—a geographical fact that largely explains the relatively indifferent British attitude. Yet German East Africa, which also fell into this geographical category, ranked high on the totem of British security. To use the old cliché, it was the 'missing link' in the chain of British possessions from the Cape to Cairo. That consideration preoccupied British statesmen during the Peace Conference as it had during the war, as is indicated from the following extract from a letter written by Harcourt to Milner:

I think I ought to warn you, as I did your two predecessors, that in the Peace settlement of German East Africa the province of Ruanda at the North-western corner of G.E.A. should on no account go to the Belgians or in any way pass out of British control. It is the only possible route for the Cape to Cairo railway, if that project is ever realized. . . .[88]

The East African problem came to a head in early May. Wilson finally yielded to the increasingly sharp demands of the southern Dominion and French delegates to assign mandatory responsibilities for the German colonies.[89] The moment was especially opportune for the British and French because of the absence during most of the meetings of the Italian Prime

[87] Memorandum by Milner, 'Cameroons and Togoland', 29 May 1919, Milner Papers.
[88] Harcourt to Milner, 13 Feb. 1919, Milner Papers. Milner replied: 'As far as I can yet judge it may be necessary to give the Belgians *something*. . . . Meanwhile, I will do my best to hold on to Ruanda'. 1 Mar. 1919, Harcourt Papers.
[89] See *Foreign Relation, Paris Peace Conference, V*, pp. 492–509.

Minister. On 8 May the press announced that the British Empire, France and Japan had become trustees of virtually all of the former German colonial empire. The Italians, Belgians and Portuguese immediately protested. Four days later Milner met with the colonial adviser to the Belgian Foreign Office, Pierre Orts, to discuss the Belgian grievance of being excluded from the East African settlement.[90] In no gentle words Milner told Orts that it was 'intolerable' that the Belgians had occupied the best part of German East Africa and had blocked the Cape to Cairo route. He argued that the extension of Belgian dominion into German East Africa was objectionable because it would violate the 'natural frontier' between east and central Africa; and he stated 'most emphatically' that the British would not tolerate the Belgians 'sitting' on their 'lines of communication from East and West and from North to South'. Orts, after considerable skirmishing, 'admitted the force' of Milner's argument. He said that his government was prepared to hand over the territory necessary for British 'communications' but that Belgium must retain most of the districts of Ruanda and Urundi. That concession satisfied Milner so far as strategic considerations were concerned, but he was far from happy about the Belgians taking over Ruanda and Urundi:

... The districts of Ruanda and Urundi, though small in extent, are in some respects the best part of all German East Africa. They are healthy highlands, very fertile, and well cultivated as East African cultivation goes. They have a very large population, something like 3 millions, which is about 40% of the total native population of German East Africa. They are also particularly rich in cattle. ...[91]

Still, Milner was willing to concede these districts to Belgium:

... I should be prepared, especially in the case of a small power like Belgium, to err if I must err on the side of generosity; and I feel that with the enormous extent of mandated territory which the Peace settlement is likely in any case to leave in our hands, we can well afford to do without Ruanda and Urundi.[92]

[90] These negotiations are examined in detail by W. R. Louis, *Ruanda-Urundi, 1884–1919* (Oxford, 1963), chap. XXI.
[91] Memorandum by Milner, 'Negotiations with Belgium about German East Africa', no date (May, 1919), Milner Papers.
[92] *Ibid.*

Milner knew, however, that the Belgians were merely using Ruanda and Urundi as a pawn. What they really wanted was not part of East Africa but a strip of territory on the south of the Congo mouth on the west coast. 'They are extremely embarrassed by the very narrow sea front of their enormous Congo territory, and by the fact that they only possess one—the Northern—bank of the Mouth of the Congo'. Milner went on:

If they could get a strip of land on the south of that river, extending as far as Ambrizette, I believe that they would be willing to give up almost the whole of Ruanda and Urundi, and this would be from every point of view the best solution.[93]

That proposed solution to the 'East African tangle' (as Milner referred to it in his diary) involved persuading the Portuguese to part with the southern bank of the Congo. They would do this only in return for a substantial *quid pro quo* elsewhere. Milner therefore proposed to give the Portuguese some territory in the south of German East Africa. In this way Belgium would receive the southern bank of the Congo river; Portugal would expand into southern German East Africa; and Britain would acquire Ruanda and Urundi. This bargain failed to materialize, however, because the Portuguese refused to be bought off, in their opinion, with worthless territory. After 'troublesome and time wasting' negotiations, in Milner's words, Belgium was left with Ruanda-Urundi,[94] as was agreed upon by Orts and Milner on 30 May 1919. Despite the protest of the American colonial representative, G. L. Beer, and of the Anti-Slavery and Aborigines Protection Society, the Milner-Orts agreement proved final.[95]

[93] *Ibid.*

[94] Except for a strip of territory in eastern Ruanda which was handed over to Belgium in 1923.

[95] At a meeting of the Mandates Commission on 16 July, Beer pointed out the Milner-Orts agreement's 'absurdity from the geographical, ethnographical and political standpoints'. He later wrote: 'This agreement cannot be defended except on grounds of merest expediency. It is contrary to the fundamental principles upon which these colonies were to be disposed of in that no attention at all was paid to native interests'. (Beer's Diary, 13 July–4 Aug. 1919). The Anti-Slavery and Aborigines Protection Society protested that 'past experience of Belgian proceedings in the Congo does not encourage an extension of the rule of that nation over large portions of Africa', and Harris complained that talk of the 'sacred trust' in this regard was 'manifest hypocrisy'. On Beer's and Harris's attempts to influence the

So far from being willing to give up the southern Congo bank for part of German East Africa, the Portuguese demanded the southern part of the latter territory as a mandate. Milner thought that this was preposterous:

The Portuguese have in my opinion no claim whatever to receive a mandate for any portion of German East Africa on the score of what they have done in the conquest of it.... they even failed to defend their own boundaries against Von Lettow, when our operations rendered his position in East Africa untenable, and by that failure prolonged the war in East Africa about a year.[96]

At a meeting of the Mandates Commission (established by the Conference to draft the mandates[97] and to study the problems of setting up the Permanent Commission) on 12 July, the Portuguese were told they could not have part of German East Africa as a mandate. To silence them they were given in full sovereignty a scrap of territory called the 'Kionga Triangle' in northern Mozambique, which rounded off the Portuguese territory at the natural frontier of the Rovuma river.[98] This was done, in Milner's words, 'as a matter of grace and convenience'.

The Portuguese were extremely suspicious of the machinations of the other imperial powers. Their suspicions were justified. At the Conference the Portuguese learned that the Italians were pressing the British to support their efforts to establish a 'trading company' in Angola. According to a British memorandum:

The Italian Delegate was unable to explain satisfactorily why the good offices of H.M.G. should be required in order to enable them to carry on trade with a Portuguese Colony. On being pressed however it appeared that the real aim was political. The Italian Delegate has now explained that Italy wishes H.M.G. to conclude with

territorial settlement, see my two articles, 'The United States and the African Peace Settlement of 1919' and 'Sir John Harris and International Trusteeship'.

[96] Memorandum by Milner, 29 May 1919, Milner Papers.

[97] On the drafting and conferring of the mandates, see my article 'South-West African Origins of the "Sacred Trust" '; and Mary Boyd, 'New Zealand's Attitude to Dominion Status, 1919–1921', *Journal of Commonwealth Political Studies*, III (March 1965).

[98] See H. B. Thomas, 'The Kionga Triangle', *Tanganyika Notes and Records*, XXXI (July 1951).

Italy an agreement similar to the secret agreement with Germany
of 1898, whereby in the event of a disruption of the Portuguese
colonial possessions part would fall to H.M.G. and part (including
Angola) to Germany.[99]

The British refused on grounds that 'Imperialism' was dead.
'Such an arrangement in the present altered state of the world',
wrote a Foreign Office official, 'would be quite unthinkable'.[1]
Though the British rebuffed Italian overtures regarding the
Portuguese colonies, they were bound by the Treaty of London
to consider the more general problem of 'equitable compensation' for Italy in Africa. On 7 May the Supreme Council
appointed an Inter-Allied Committee composed of Milner,
Simon and an Italian delegate, Silvio Crespi, to discuss Italian
territorial claims, which extended over a large part of north-
eastern Africa. Most of the regions claimed by Italy were, as
Milner described them, 'mainly desert'; but even so the British
and the French were reluctant to hand them over to the
Italians. The remarkable feature that struck Milner about
Italian ambitions was the extent to which they involved British
territory: 'from the first it was Great Britain that was asked to
make the principal sacrifices'. He went on:

In Libya the area claimed from Great Britain was three or four
times as large as that claimed from France. ... In asking for the
whole of British and French Somaliland, Italy was asking us to
give up a country ten times as large as France was asked to give up.
Finally in Jubaland the territory asked for by Italy was exclusively
British.[2]

Milner was willing only to make a rectification of the Libyan
frontier in Italy's favour and to cede the region in the north
of British East Africa called the Jubaland valley—which he
described as 'a fertile district capable of growing large quanti-

[99] Italy similarly demanded a 'free hand' to trade in Abyssinia. 'In this
matter as in others the Italian Government are using trade as a cloak for
political aims'. R. Sperling memorandum, 11 Mar. 1919, Lothian Papers.
[1] *Ibid.* On Italian colonial aims in the First World War, see Robert L.
Hess, 'Italy and Africa: Colonial Ambitions in the First World War',
Journal of African History, IV (1963). For Italian colonial negotiations at the
Peace Conference, René Albrecht-Carrié, *Italy at the Paris Peace Conference*
(New York, 1938), chap. VIII.
[2] Memorandum by Milner, ' "Equitable Compensation" for Italy in
Africa', 30 May 1919, Milner Papers.

ties of cotton'. In Somaliland Milner 'declined to budge' on grounds that Britain had already given away more than France. He did not see 'why we should continue to make all the sacrifices'. In fact he wanted to yield as little as possible:

I may say I was rather glad that the French took up an uncompromising attitude about Jibuti (French Somaliland), as, if they had been more yielding about it, I might have found it difficult to refuse Berbera [in British Somaliland] and the part of British Somaliland adjoining it.

'Ultimately I presume', Milner wrote, 'Italy will have to be satisfied with what France and Great Britain are prepared to give up'.[3] The main points of the final settlement included only the cession of the Juba valley by Britain and a few oases in the Sahara by France.[4]

This niggardly attitude of Britain and France was largely determined by the putative strategic importance of north-eastern Africa and the unsettled state of affairs in Abyssinia. According to Milner: 'as long as the fate of Abyssinia, which is one of the most serious international problems of the near future, remains undecided, neither France, Italy nor England can be expected to give up any positions now held by them, from which they can exercise an influence on the future of that country.'[5] At the bottom of the Abyssinian problem was the question of the Nile.

We . . . have one absolutely vital interest; it is to safeguard the head waters of the Blue Nile. . . . When the time comes to liquidate the Abyssinian situation, we must be in a position to stipulate for the security of this water supply.[6]

. . . It is vitally important to Egypt to retain undisputed control of the Nile.[7]

As in the days of Lord Salisbury, British statesmen at the Peace Conference believed that the power in possession of the Nile valley controlled Egypt and the route to India. By the end of

[3] *Ibid.* See also Milner's memorandum in Lloyd George, *The Truth about the Peace Treaties*, II, 898-901.
[4] See Hess, 'Italy and Africa'.
[5] Memorandum by Milner, ' "Equitable Compensation" for Italy in Africa', 30 May 1919, Milner Papers.
[6] *Ibid.*
[7] Memorandum by R. Sperling, 11 Mar. 1919, Lothian Papers.

the First World War the ramifications of Salisbury's Nile policy had led Britain into a large part of the Middle East and German East Africa as the 'mandatory power'. Even in the disposal of the former German West African colonies, protection of the 'other' route to India was a primary consideration. As Balfour once said: 'every time I come to a discussion—at intervals of, say, five years—I find there is a new sphere which we have got to guard, which is supposed to protect the gateways of India. Those gateways are getting farther and farther from India'.[8]

Apart from the representatives of the southern Dominions, British statesmen in 1919 did not regard the establishment of the mandates system as a threat to the security of India or of the Empire as a whole. Nor did the apportionment of the mandates greatly affect the partition of Africa. As in the Pacific the continent was divided mainly along the lines of conquest. To the regret of the British delegates at the Peace Conference, there was little room for manoeuver. According to Lord Robert Cecil: 'I know that if Mr. Balfour or myself makes any proposition with regard to Africa, we shall be told that it is the oldest colony, or it will bitterly offend some New Zealand politician if we do it, or something of that kind. It is always the same'.[9] So also did the First World War end in the same way as other wars—in Balfour's words, with a 'map of the world with more red on it'. In his opinion the reason was geographical. But the expansion of the British Empire, he said, 'might not be ascribed in other countries to its geographical cause'.[10] Whatever its cause, imperialism at the Peace Conference was not easy to disguise, even by the founding of the mandates system. The fate of the German colonies was determined, in Milner's frank opinion, by a 'huge scramble'. From their superior geographical position the British merely led the race.

*   *   *

The colonial aims of Great Britain differed fundamentally from those of the European powers mainly because of the size and nature of the British Empire. Britain's strength and the

[8] Eastern Committee Minutes, Secret, 9 Dec. 1918, CAB. 27/24.
[9] Ibid.
[10] Ibid., 24 Apr. 1918.

threats to her security were world-wide. None of the continental states could draw upon military support from white Dominions as well as Asian and African colonies; and no other power was as dependent as Britain on distant markets and sources of supply connected with the mother country by life lines of communication vulnerable to attack by naval raiders and submarines. Fortunately for Britain, Germany had made little use before the war of overseas territories for naval bases. Admiral von Tirpitz, the builder of the German navy, believed in the *grande guerre* and not in the *guerre de course*. He concentrated on the battle fleet in the North Sea and neglected chances of commerce raiding in a war against Britain. There were no submarines based in the colonies. In the war itself the German army command confined naval operations mainly to European waters, where the battle fleet proved too weak for victory. Yet German submarines in 1917 nearly destroyed Britain's command of the seas. British statesmen calculated that if the Germans had possessed more submarines, and had established bases in overseas colonies, the British merchant marine could have been destroyed and Britain might have been starved into submission. So real did that danger seem during the war that the British were determined that Germany should never again have colonial naval bases where submarines could threaten their lines of communication with the overseas empire. By absorbing most of the German colonies into the Empire, and by extending British influence into the Middle East, British leaders intended to lay a basis for continuous overland communication from southern Africa through Egypt to India, thereby consolidating the 'Southern British World'. After a war in which German submarines had nearly brought Britain to her knees, long stretches of territory for continuous air and land communication seemed to be a prerequisite for future security.

Britain's Empire, with its bases of power in southern Africa, India, Australasia and North America, stood out in striking contrast to the empires of the western European states. With the exception of the Dutch, those empires were essentially African, some having important supplements in other parts of the world. The colonial goals of the belligerent continental powers accordingly developed in relation to African colonies that would form a base for expansion and consolidation, and in relation to the region that forms the bridge between Europe, Africa, and Asia—the Middle East. Thus the natural course for German expansion in Africa seemed to be through the Belgian Congo and the Portuguese colonies, which, if brought under German sway, would link German East Africa with the Cameroons and South-West Africa. For France, with vast possessions in the north and west of Africa, the acquisition of German colonial territory would consolidate French power in a region stretching from the Mediterranean to the Gulf of Guinea. The minor belligerents also tried to augment their colonial empires and to make boundary rectifications and other adjustments to improve the efficiency of their colonial administrations. The Belgians aimed mainly at strengthening their hold over the mouth of the Congo river; the Portuguese wanted to round off their sphere in East Africa and vainly hoped to extend it substantially into the neighbouring German colony; and the Italians dreamed of an enlarged empire in northeastern Africa as well as in the Balkans and Asia Minor. The lesser European powers did not realize their principal ambitions, but each held on to whatever new territory it had acquired because it would have been humiliating to emerge empty-handed from the scramble for spoils. Colonial gains, however trivial, were a tangible proof of victory.

As in earlier wars, Britain's general war aims as well as her colonial ambitions differed substantially from those of the European powers. The preoccupation of most continental statesmen was with European security and possible territorial and economic expansion in Europe itself. Britain, on the other hand, fought not only for specific European goals such as the liberation of Belgium and the destruction of 'Prussian militarism' but also for the security of her empire throughout the world.[11] To European and American eyes the 'British Empire', with its seat of government in London, appeared as a monolithic political body whose voracious territorial appetite satisfied itself in Asia,

[11] The best recent discussions of general war aims are by Fischer, *Griff nach der Weltmacht*; Gerhard Ritter, *Staatskunst und Kriegshandwerk: Das Problem des Militarismus in Deutschland*, vol. 3, *Die Tragödie der Staatskunst: Bethmann Hollweg als Kriegskanzler, 1914–17* (Munich, 1964); Hans W. Gatzke, *Germany's Drive to the West* (Baltimore, 1950); Pierre Renouvin, 'Les buts de guerre du gouvernement français (1914–18)', *Revue Historique*, CCXXXV (Jan.–Mar. 1966); and A. J. P. Taylor, 'The War Aims of the Allies in the First World War', in *Politics in Wartime* (London, 1964).

the Middle East, and Africa; and to some observers the British no less and possibly more than the Germans were thus guilty of pursuing a policy of *Weltpolitik*. While Britain's allies fought for their survival on the continent, the indictment ran, Britain herself, as in the past, was left free to acquire large parts of the non-European world. Lloyd George and other British statesmen countered this charge by pointing out that most of the colonial conquests were made by the Dominions, which, though nominally not yet sovereign, had passed beyond the control of London. It would have been impossible in 1919 for Britain to block Australia's acquisition of New Guinea in the same way that the Colonial Office had done in 1883 when Queensland had attempted to annex that territory. The phrase 'British Empire', with its implication of central authority and control, nevertheless engendered suspicion and bitterness among allies and enemies alike. The cooperation of Britain and the Dominions at the Peace Conference and later in the League of Nations strengthened the impression that the Empire was a single unit. Actually the political complexion of the Empire at this time was like a kaleidoscope, its colours changing according to the opportunities and demands of the moment. It was at once an Empire and a group of separate and almost sovereign states.

British statesmen did not deny Germany her colonies primarily for economic reasons. Nor did the British public regard tropical Africa as a potentially rich field for exploitation as had been envisaged during the 'scramble' of the 1880s and 1890s. In the earlier period much of the territory parcelled out among the European powers was unexplored. What was unknown, so the logic ran, might contain great deposits of mineral or other natural wealth, or might provide vast markets for European goods. As late as the Peace Conference a few statesmen of the jingo school continued to look upon African colonies as 'undeveloped estates'. But on the whole the illusions of tropical paradises had been dispelled by the time of the First World War, and dismal calculations of the cost and trouble of assuming more territorial responsibilities had to be counterbalanced by optimistic estimates of the strategic value of colonies. Paradoxically the vision of overseas wealth did materialize later: in the interwar years the oil of the Middle East and the minerals and other raw materials of Africa gave previously neglected territories an immense importance in the world's economy; and Africa's economic development coincided with the main period of European settlement. In an era of tariff barriers and restrictive immigration, many white settlers hoped to find in Africa the opportunity no longer possible in the more developed parts of the world. In Germany colonial enthusiasts demanded the return of the 'lost colonies' to relieve population pressure and to provide overseas markets and raw materials. They were restrained by Hitler, who interpreted the loss of the colonies in a different way. He condemned Bismarck for making the German empire vulnerable to attack by the British navy. Under the Nazis the forces behind the German imperialism that had built a colonial empire in Africa and Asia were channelled in another direction. *Weltpolitik* became *Ostpolitik*, that is, expansion on the European continent towards the east. In 1938 the British, in the tradition of attempting to achieve European peace by bartering colonial territories, offered to redraw the map of tropical Africa to Germany's advantage (and presumably at Belgium's and Portugal's expense). Hitler refused to listen. Unlike the Germans of Wilhelmian times, the Nazis could not be bought off with strips of African jungle.

The scramble for overseas territories that President Wilson regarded as a threat to the peace of the world was not in a strict sense a scramble at all but the simple take-over of enemy possessions. After the conquest of the German colonies, the occupying powers then debated whether those territories should be permanently retained. Economic considerations played an important role in these deliberations—as in 1919 when Smuts, lamenting that the British Empire was 'specially poor in copper', urged not only that most of the German colonies should be retained but also that part of Portuguese and Belgian Africa should be acquired.[12] But, contrary to the school of economic determinism, the reasons for the decision to keep Germany's colonies was not primarily economic. The powerful theme of *Africa and the Victorians* is even more true of British statesmen of the First World War period than for those of the partition era: 'Over and over again, they show an obsession with security, a fixation of safeguarding the routes to the East.'[13]

[12] Memorandum by Smuts, 'The Mozambique Province', Very Secret, n.d. (Jan. 1919), Smuts Papers.   [13] *Africa and the Victorians*, p. 470.

If the retention of Germany's overseas possessions seemed necessary for the defence of the Empire, it was not only the territory and resources which were worth defending but also the idea of British civilization. The British statesmen who wanted to paint more of the map red did so in the conviction that British rule over Africans and Asians was superior to Germany's, and that continued German control of the colonies would endanger the peace of the world. To most Englishmen, the theory of 'mandates' merely embodied sound principles of British colonial rule. There is surely as much truth in that view as in the aphorism that imperialism wore an increasingly elaborate fig-leaf.

The First World War was the first fought between industrial powers dependent in various degrees on overseas territories and sources of supply, the first involving democratic states responsive to public opinion and the idea of protecting 'backward peoples', and the first in which defence of democracy became inseparable from the defence of empire. The ideas of empire and democracy are not always compatible, as President Wilson pointed out in 1919. He wanted colonial subjects to be consulted about their fate. He asked for a fair colonial settlement in which 'the interests of the populations concerned must have equal weight with the equitable claims of the governments whose title is to be determined'. His plea reflected the belief that Africans and Asians should and eventually would determine their own future. His voice was prophetic. During the collapse of the great colonial empires of western Europe little more than a quarter of a century later, Africans and Asians used many of the same arguments that the British had used against German colonial rule. They invoked above all President Wilson's principle embodied in Article 22 of the League Covenant—the right 'to stand by themselves'.

INDEX

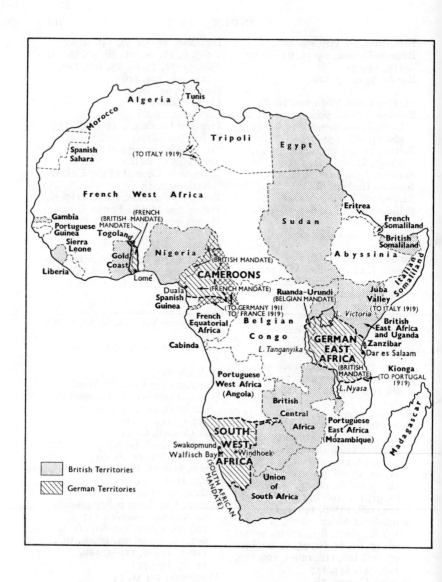

Morocco

Algeria   Tunis

Spanish
Sahara   (TO ITALY 1919)

Tripoli

Egypt

French   West   Africa

Sudan

Eritrea

French
Somaliland

Gambia   (FRENCH
Portuguese   MANDATE)
Guinea   (BRITISH
          MANDATE)
Sierra   Togoland
Leone
            Gold
            Coast
Liberia   Lomé

Nigeria

(BRITISH MANDATE)

CAMEROONS
      (FRENCH MANDATE)
Duala
Spanish
Guinea   (TO GERMANY 1911
            TO FRANCE 1919)
      French
      Equatorial   Belgian
      Africa

Ruanda-Urundi
(BELGIAN MANDATE)

British
Somaliland

A b y s s i n i a

Juba
Valley
(TO ITALY 1919)

L. Victoria   British
               East Africa
               and Uganda

Cabinda   Congo

L. Tanganyika

GERMAN
EAST
AFRICA

Zanzibar
Dar es Salaam

Kionga
(TO PORTUGAL
1919)

Portuguese
West Africa
(Angola)

British
Central
Africa

(BRITISH
MANDATE)
L. Nyasa

Portuguese
East Africa
(Mozambique)

Madagascar

Swakopmund
Walfisch Bay

SOUTH-
WEST
AFRICA
(SOUTH AFRICAN
MANDATE)

*Windhoek

Union
of
South Africa

British Territories

German Territories

British Territories

German Territories

CHINA

Kiaochow

JAPAN

Mariana Is.

FRENCH
INDO-CHINA

Philippine
Is.

(JAPANESE MANDATES)

Yap

Palau Is.

Caroline Is.

Marshall Is.

GERMAN
NEW GUINEA

Equator

DUTCH EAST INDIES

DUTCH
NEW GUINEA

Bismarck Arch.
(AUST.
MANDATE)

Rabaul

Nauru (BRITISH MANDATE)

Solomon Is.

Papua
(Aust.)

Samoa
(N.Z.
MANDATE)

New Hebrides
(ANGLO FRENCH
CONDOMINIUM)

A U S T R A L I A

NEW
ZEALAND